Shotgunner
Reflections on Birds, Guns, and Dogs

Shotgunner
Reflections on Birds, Guns, and Dogs

by

Steve Smith

Illustrated
by Christopher S. Smith

Wilderness
Adventures
Press

Gallatin Gateway, Montana

Text © 1998 Steve Smith
Artwork © 1998 Christopher S. Smith

Published by Wilderness Adventures Press
P.O. Box 627
Gallatin Gateway, MT 59730
800-925-3339

10 9 8 7 6 5 4 3 2 1

Printed in the United States of America

Library of Congress Cataloging-in-Publication Data:

Smith, Steve, 1947–
    Shotgunner : reflections on birds, guns, and dogs / Steve Smith : illustrated by Christopher S. Smith.
        p.   cm.
    ISBN 1-885106-66-1 (alk. paper). – – ISBN 1-885106-67-X (alk. paper)
    1. Fowling.   2. Shotguns   3. Birds dogs.   I. Title.
SK313.S55   1998
799.2'4– –dc21   98-34932
                                                                    CIP

For Hilly

Table of Contents

Introduction

THOSE FEW OF YOU KIND ENOUGH to buy this book will read of the little I know about shotguns and shooting. I'm not the best shot in the world or the most expert about shotguns, probably ranking at the fiftieth percentile or a bit less in both categories.

But as you'll be able to see as you read this, I love shotguns and wingshooting. I love the dogs and the country and the far-off places. I also love the friends and family who share that life with me. When you read this and you see that I talk about this or that gun or place I've been, you may get the mistaken notion that I am wealthy, a notion my banker—if he even knew who I was—would laugh himself sick over. The reality is, I am rather single-minded when it comes to this way of life, so every extra nickel I've ever earned has been spent on guns and dogs and going places to use them.

I'd like to thank the people who made this book possible, including the magazines in which some of these pieces first appeared— *Shooting Sportsman, The Pointing Dog Journal, Game & Gun, The Retriever Journal, Ducks Unlimited,* and *Petersen's Shotgun.*

I'd also like to thank a fine artist and wonderful companion, my son Chris, for the use of his pencil and pen sketches. Chris is the finest game shot I know, and the most complete waterfowler and upland hunter I've had the pleasure to meet. He and I and my other son, Jason, have spent more time and money than any of us would like to think about traveling here and there and getting wet and cold and skunked. I only hope we can do it for a whole lot longer.

Steve Smith
Traverse City, Michigan

The Guns

My Favorite Gauge

IT HAS TAKEN A LOT OF YEARS to finally arrive at my conclusions about gauges. Each of the familiar gauges — 28, 20, 16, and 12 — has plenty to offer the shooter. Most of us specialize in one kind of upland hunting, depending upon region, and therefore specialize with one gun. If you are an Eastern grouse and woodcock hunter exclusively, you may have picked a 20-gauge years ago and swore anything else was window dressing; if your hunting is almost totally Nebraska pheasants, you think anything but a 12 is effete.

Shotgunning is nothing if not traditional, and each gauge has its traditions and its followers. Most of us get our traditions from those who taught us to hunt or those with whom we hunt — fathers, brothers, friends. The choice of action — double vs. a repeating gun, maybe — always seems to be the most debated point. Gauge doesn't matter as often. Ask a gaggle of South Dakota pheasant hunters about their pet bird guns, and you'll hear about the merits of autoloaders over pumps, or maybe how over-unders seem to point with more precision than side-by-sides against an open sky, and they'll all trot out their favorite 12-gauges to prove their points.

When I was a kid, like most of you, I started off with a 20 — a single barrel with a hammer — and then a 20 double. But I couldn't wait until I had the size and the cash to get what the fast crowd liked for our Midwestern pheasants: a 12-gauge. I gravitated toward a Model 12 like my father's, but none was to be had new, and after five years of hand-me-down shotguns, I wanted a new one. Finally, when I was 17, I had saved enough money for a Winchester (a little brand loyalty thanks to the Model 12) autoloader. Cost me ninety-nine bucks, and I could make it sound like a chain saw when a bird got up. But, most important, it was a 12. It was years before I realized that a .470 nitro express elephant cartridge fired precisely one inch behind a crossing rooster pheasant had no effect, while an ounce of 6s or 7½s, placed in the head and neck at anything inside 40 yards, was a lightning strike. It was years after that before I realized that it didn't seem to make a difference to the pheasant if that ounce of shot came from a 12, a 16, or a 20.

But over the years, I have developed some particular ideas about gauges, and I have come up with my all-time, all-around favorite gauge shotgun, the one that I like the best and plan to hunt with to the exclusion of everything else. Here it is, and here are my reasons. Maybe you'll agree.

The 28-Gauge

The 28-gauge is my all-time favorite. The 28 is the grouse gun of William Harnden Foster; it is the gun of the purest of the pure purist woodcock hunters; it is a Southern dove field bathed in the lazy rays of a September sunset. To some, it is something of an "image" gun.

But practically, the 28 has a lot going for it to make it my favorite— as it should be yours. First, the gun is ballistically efficient, much more like a 20 than the .410 it is often compared with (as an aside, the .410 is a caliber, a crippler, made originally from a rifle cartridge, and an abomination. Save it for skeet). The ¾-ounce shot load is balanced with the bore diameter to produce a short shot string in relation to the pattern spread—more like a pie plate than a sausage shape going through the air. Short shot strings allow more of the shot to get to the target at the same time, increasing shocking power and therefore efficiency.

The gauge has light recoil, a good selection of loads, and the guns themselves are made up to light weights. A 28 double has slim barrels and carries like a princess. That's why it's my favorite gauge.

The 20-Gauge

The 20-gauge is my all-time favorite. The 20 is a Minnesota ruffed grouse hammering up through the aspens, an exploding covey of Georgia bobwhites, trophy pheasants flushing ahead of a slow-working shorthair, a boy's first step into manhood. The fact is, there are certain circles where shooting anything other (certainly larger) than a 20 is considered a social error—swanky Southern quail plantations leap to mind.

Twenties are my favorite guns because they are handsome, ballistically efficient, snappy handling little shotguns that carry light and shoot hard. They come in about the widest choice of actions, models, and barrel lengths of any shotgun in this country. When Parker Reproductions and the A.H. Fox Company both started making these fine guns again (Parker some years ago, Fox just recently), it was no coincidence that the gauge they introduced first was the 20.

But the 20 is no toy, as legions of shooters will testify. The loads range from 2½-inch, ¾-ounce powder puffs, to three-inch magnum, copper-plated Roman candles that could stop a lion in close. Between these, there are hard loads, soft loads, fast loads, slow loads, spreader loads, ⅞-ounce, 1-ounce, and 1⅛-ounce loads of everything from 2s to 9s. And, you can get most of these—or everything you'll need, really—from the local Wal-Mart or a backwoods Maine general store.

Efficient, traditional, available. That's why the 20 is my favorite gauge.

The 16-Gauge

The 16-gauge is my all-time favorite. The 16 is a throwback, back to the time when it was the Queen of the Uplands, tucked under the arm of a necktied gent following his Gordon setter through the woodcock alders that grew hard against a forgotten orchard on a New England hillside.

For years, the 16 was the pure upland hunter's gun: The 20 was for women and kids, the 12 for waterfowl. It was also for the aging hunter, the one for whom a heavy bag was not important anymore, but a shooter who wanted the feel of a small-bore with the authority of a 12. In fact, this gun once called the "queen of the uplands," was said to "carry like a 20 and shoot like a 12." To many people, including me, it is the essence of "shotgun." A one-ounce load of hard shot, fired through the 16-gauge barrel, just may be the most efficient shot charge in all of shotgunning, for the 16-gauge itself was so named because it takes 16 lead balls each the size of the bore to total a pound, so each ball weighs $\frac{1}{16}$ of a pound: one ounce. Because of this efficiency, it is the big-bore small gauge. Or maybe the small-bore big gauge. In any event, with a 16, you're never overgunned or undergunned.

The models available are mostly from the past of a simpler time: Parkers, Foxes, Smiths, British, and Continental makes. The 16 is a real wingshooter's gun. That's why it's my favorite.

The 12-Gauge

The 12-gauge is my all-time favorite. The 12 is authority itself, able to fold up the highest pheasant or a wild-flushing sharptail better than any other bore. The 12 is driven grouse shoots in England, a London sidelock Best gun, Nash Buckingham's "Bo Whoop," blocking a fencerow in the South Dakota Soil Bank days, and pulling a pair of Huns from a crossing covey at an honest 45 yards.

Of all the gauges, the 12 has the greatest variety. There are five-pound guns specially made for the British 2-inch 12-gauge shotshell, and old A.H. Fox "SuperFox" overbored 12s with 32-inch barrels and the reach of the IRS. The choice of shot sizes and loads is unsurpassed, perhaps more combinations than the rest of the gauges put together, when you factor in target loads. The guns themselves can be whatever your pocketbook and taste can conjure up, in any action, barrel length, weight, stock type, and trigger choice.

The 12 also has the capacity for the most efficient pattern, because the larger shot load allows a shooter to open the chokes, giving more pattern area but still retaining enough density to kill cleanly. Where a 20 might have to be bored modified for pheasants over dogs, a 12 can do it with loose improved cylinder. Inversely, tighter chokes allow the shooter an extra few yards in range over the other gauges, a bonus for the middle-aged shooter whose hearing and intensity might not keep him on that razor's edge he once trod when he was younger, a few thousand shots ago.

That's why the 12 is my favorite.

The Complete Battery

THERE'S BEEN A LOT WRITTEN about the sort and number of guns we should have in our cabinet, the gauge and barrel length and weight and fit of each, and their uses. God knows, I've written enough of it myself.

But the best explanation for those of us who have more guns than we can use is the shooting-is-a-whole-lot-like-golf rationale.

We know golf is a game of distances and weather and topography, like shooting. We also know pivot and balance and follow-through and smoothness are necessary in both sports.

So, if a golfer feels it necessary to carry a legal maximum of 14 clubs, why can't we have 14 shotguns? Okay, what about 10?

I was telling this to the Storm and Strife the other day, because I'd just picked up a new little French guild gun, a light 12 made in the '30s, and explained its finer points and what work I was having done on it right then. I hadn't quite got around to telling her that the work would cost about what I paid for the gun originally, but I figured that was better discussed at another time, like when the bank statement came in.

She asked what I was planning to use this gun for, and I said that up until I got it, I had really felt inadequate and frankly a bit embarrassed on Huns and sharptails in the West, especially on days when they came off the ground at 40 yards and I was hunting with people who were good shots who knew the birds and that I felt, really, it was hurting my social standing, all that missing and cursing.

She wanted to know how many days I hunted Huns and sharptails in the West in an average year, and I told her probably five or six. I managed to get her away from the long division concerning the cost-per-day of the gun over the next 10 years if I used it just for the purpose I intended by mentioning how I loved the way the afternoon sun glinted off her graying hair.

But it got me to thinking, the golf club hypothesis aside, about how many guns really are enough.

Since most of us hunt one species of game or shoot in one set of conditions almost exclusively, the guns we accumulate, as I said earlier, seem to resemble each other. If you are a grouse and woodcock hunter and practically live in the alder swamps and aspen whips, you may have over-unders, side-bys, or maybe even a light little auto. But I'm willing to bet if you pick up anything besides a 20, it's a 28. And it's light.

Or if you figure the only sort of bird worth squinting at down a gun barrel is a ringneck, your guns, I'm willing to bet, have long barrels, tight chokes, and have "12" stamped all over them.

But that's no reason to ignore the Wonderful World of Other Guns You Ought to Have. First, in order to feel fully clothed, you should have a light brush gun. I don't think the ultralight, short-barreled numbers passed off as brush guns are right, and I like barrels of at least 26 inches,

Mr. Churchill's XXV notwithstanding. There has to be a certain amount of weight in order to stabilize the mounting procedure—an ultralight gun just bounces too much, and by the time you get the bouncing stopped, the bird—grouse, woodcock, or thick-country quail—is gone. Anything under 5½ pounds is just too light for me; maybe it's different for you. Our brush gun can be, practically, any gauge we want. The ranges are normally short and the birds fragile. I know good shots who carry light 12s and 28s interchangeably, and it doesn't seem to matter. A woodcock at 18 yards isn't exactly a Cape buffalo at 75.

Chokes? I think we're looking at a light improved cylinder and a loose modified. Some quick shots go with cylinder or skeet, especially if they are using a bigger bore—16 or 12—and have the luxury of being able to densify the pattern with an ounce of shot or a tad more.

Next, if you do a wide variety of hunting, you should have a prairie gun of some kind, maybe a late-season gun. The name isn't important, but the configuration is. I've found that a light 12 of 6½ pounds or so makes the miles shorter. But it should have the ability to reach out, so we're talking tight chokes. I have one, the second of a nearly identical pair of 12s, that's 6¼ pounds, choked modified and full, a combination of fairly light weight coupled with authority.

But with such a light gun comes the problem of recoil. I get the shakes from shooting heavy loads in a light gun like everyone else, but our prairie gun (or late-season pheasant gun or whatever) is normally carried a whole lot more than it's shot—aren't they all?—so a shot every mile or so won't make you start flinching and drooling at the corner of the mouth.

But still, a light gun should be given a diet of light loads, if for no other reason than the integrity of the gun. I like the 2½-inch shells made in the States by a couple of companies or imported from England. In 12-gauge, these shells pack a nice punch, have a short shot string, and handle pheasants about as well as anything—provided you do your part and don't risk long shots and stay very head-conscious as you shoot.

Chokes? As I alluded to above, tight. Modified and full or improved cylinder and full, a nice combination, are about right. I like the barrels long—28 inches, 30 if I could get them.

Okay, so that's the brush gun and prairie gun—I know, bad names, but you get the idea. That obviously leaves us needing only a waterfowl gun. And here, because of present steel shot restrictions, the bottom starts to fall out. Steel shot means heavy, thick barrels. The velocity at which steel shot needs to be flung out there into the wild blue also means stout frames, so a slim-wristed double is out of the question.

Bismuth shot, being about as malleable as lead and therefore not harmful to barrels, will attenuate the thick-barrel problem, but bismuth starts off with a pretty good whack as well, partly because it is less dense than lead (though more so than steel) and needs a lot of front-end oompha to achieve killing penetrations downrange. Tungsten shot has great penetration, but it's as hard as steel.

In any event, waterfowling today means—and really always has— a big gun: big frame, lots of weight, long barrels. Here, our thoughtful shotgunner may well find that any of the pumps or autoloaders on the market today will serve him well. My preference is for pumps because I think you can treat them a little rougher and get away with it, and waterfowling is a tough sport. But I'm sure that's prejudice. Today's autoloaders are really pretty idiot-proof. One piece of advice: With three shots available to you, save that third round to anchor a cripple on the water. Studies have shown that, too often, the third shot from a repeating gun fired at birds in the air is the crippler. By the time you've fired the first two, most times the birds have flared and turned, putting distance and shielding bone and feathers between you and their vital head/neck area where clean kills are made.

So, how do we get the 14 shotguns we need? Well, each of these guns I've described should have a backup in case of damage or malfunction during the shooting season.

And, certain conditions mean certain, specialized pieces. Like, have you got a really good rainy-day-ahead-of-a-wide-ranging-pointer-in-the-mesquite quail gun?

The mind reels.

Fallen Lady Revisited

IN HAVILAH BABCOCK'S SUPERB story "Fallen Lady," he recounts a bittersweet escapade in which he found *the* quail gun—one that fit him to perfection, one with which he could not miss, and one that, at first, he cannot own, because the man who does is making too much money renting it to him throughout the quail season.

Havilah finally acquires the gun at a staggering price and finds, upon seriously cleaning it up for the first time, that the cheap barrel blacking covers…Damascus steel. He attempts to shoot the gun, but fear of imminent barrel-rupture ruins his shooting and his days afield—every time he shoots it, he stops and counts his fingers. He tries to have the gun's stock measurements translated into the wood of another, safer gun—no good. Finally, he puts the gun away—in his attic, I think—and periodically he rediscovers it and sits with it awhile…and remembers.

Babcock had no choice—his was a safety consideration. But there was another lesson here: He didn't care how the gun looked or its make; he could shoot it well and that was what counted.

What about us, where do we stand on "beauty is as beauty does"?

We all like to own, carry, shoot, and fondle our best guns. When we're in the company of other shooters who feel the same way, it's fun to look at each other's guns, swing them, and imagine ourselves knocking cold the driven pheasant, rocketing partridge, or clattering quail. The past few seasons, the folks I hunted with trotted out for inspection, variously: Woodwards, Purdeys, Hollands, Scotts, Beretta EELLs, Parkers, and the odd C Grade Fox or two. Gorgeous guns, all.

But of these people, more than half of them admitted—along with me—that the gun they shot the best wasn't with them right then; it was home in the gun cabinet. They didn't want to produce the real shooters because they might be embarrassed in such company. The leave-at-homes included: Fox Sterlingworths, Parker Trojans, a Winchester 24, a couple of Belgian guild guns, and my old French gun whose name I've been able to neither decipher nor detect.

Like Babcock's Fallen Lady, this gun doesn't give anyone the chills. I picked it up used for a song about 10 years ago. At first description, it sounds fairly nice: 6½ pounds and balanced a tad barrel-heavy, straight stock bent for me, splinter forend, double triggers set for 3 and 3¾ pounds. The chambers are 2½ inches, and I shoot one-ounce English loads. The fastening is about the strongest I've ever seen—rib extension, third grip and all—and doesn't even hint at looseness, even though the gun was probably made in the early '50s and looks like it's been rode hard and put up wet; the top lever is still dead-center or a degree or two to the right. The barrels are 27½ inches, and the rib is swamped to the point that it's hardly even there, giving me a delightful sight picture.

That's the good news. The bad news is, it has no ejectors, the stock looks like it was whittled from barrel staves, the engraving was probably hand-done blindfolded and probably by a drunk, and the blueing is a distant memory.

And when I get together with people who know guns to do a little shooting, there's always a bit of strained silence when I produce my little marvel. Nobody really wants to say anything, but the clearing of throats, shuffling of feet, and sidelong glances speak volumes.

Until I shoot it. You see, like Fallen Lady, this is one of those guns that maybe only happens once in a lifetime. Let me explain.

I'm not sure what my 35-year average is on grouse, woodcock, pheasants, and quail, the upland birds I hunt the most religiously, but I can assure you that I have never heard the phrase: "…reincarnation of Bogardus" uttered anywhere in my vicinity. Years ago, I used to track shooting averages—birds per shell—but I got out of the habit when it appeared things weren't going to get any better than they were, and I really didn't want to know if they were getting worse.

But then I got this gun and had a little work done on it, more like a winter project to putter with as much as anything—we've all done it. I started to get the idea that maybe something was up when I went through the woodcock season and didn't miss a bird. Now, I normally and purposely shoot only two or three of the five allowed by law where I live, and back then only over the points my old girl of a setter gave me. We'd sort of putter along, neither of us out there to break any kind of records. Certainly, we both lacked a little of the fire we did when we were a dozen years younger. So, I had a tendency to pick my shots, which is more fun and makes me look good, but that year I even made a couple of hard tries.

Grouse were a bit more difficult, but still the average was, for me, unbelievable and therefore unprintable. Then I went to Iowa for a week on pheasants and quail. Again, the average was way over my lifetime high. At the end of the upland season, my shooting average on all birds/all shots, hovered right at 90 percent! Then the waterfowl season kicked in, I switched to a steel shot gun, and my shooting fell off to its normal average, just this side of abysmal.

In short, there was no epiphany in technique; not likely to be, either, given my age and number of years spent getting grooved in my faults. No, it was the gun. It had to be the gun!

So what do we do? What works out to perfect is having a great gun, one we're proud of, that we shoot like it's an extension of our psyche. What often happens is the gun we like the best, we can't shoot, and the one we'd like to hide from our accomplices is like my particular Fallen Lady—we just have a hard time missing with it. Like Babcock, we can have the fit translated into another gun, which won't work any better for us than it did for him. Or we can use it when the prying eyes of our betters aren't around. Or we can gulp hard and shoot it and let the final result speak for us and for itself. Tough decisions.

We don't like to admit it, but a lot of the reason we buy, collect, trade, and keep moving guns around is to impress our playmates. I've got a close friend who, annually in the spring, drives me and everyone around him into a stark-raving frenzy because he gets "newgunitis." He calls England and France and Spain and Italy. He collects catalogs, bugs importers and dealers, and eventually comes up with what he wants—his "perfect" gun.

And part of his decision-making process about what is this year's perfect gun is the name. For years, he said something like, "The name doesn't matter—if it's a Best grade gun made especially for me with my choice of engraving, stock, and the rest of it, I'll know it; so what if the guys I shoot with don't appreciate it?" Turns out it does matter, and the guns he ends up considering have the names we could all recite in our sleep. He just likes shooting a gun bearing the name of a recognizable Best gunmaker.

His conundrum is made a little easier by the fact that he's a good shot and can shoot anything pretty well. But last year, while he was thinking up a likely candidate for Perfect Gun, Episode IX, he was caught without a gun to actually shoot (he hadn't really thought about that part of it). So he took an old one out of the gun cabinet, a gun he shot as a boy, a 16-gauge Savage. He sent it off to have the stock lengthened and bent, the chokes opened, the pistol grip removed, and the triggers tuned. He shot it all season. He shot it better than he ever shot anything else in his life, too, to hear him tell it, and if he had to toss it down while he chased down one of his semitrained mutts or use it to hold down a strand of barbed wire while he ambled over, it didn't matter.

Now my pal has his own Fallen Lady, his own little 16-bore enigma. You see, he loved shooting and hitting and not worrying about the gun, and he loved how his friends took less notice of his fowling piece and more notice of the frequency with which the fowl hit the ground.

So what does he do this spring? He calls and tells me that even though he really enjoyed last season, he can't see hunting with anything less than a London Best, so he ordered one. It'll be here in two years.

Says I:"What will you do in the meantime?"

"I'll just have to make do with my Savage."

I could hear him chuckle as he hung up the phone. You see, he's solved the problem: He can shoot the gun he shoots best and not feel ashamed because he's got the Best gun on order.

And if it takes four years instead of two to get here…oh well.

To Shoot or Not To Shoot

ONE OF THE GREAT PROBLEMS facing those of you who own fine guns is the recurring dilemma of whether or not to shoot them, to use them as they were intended when they were built a half-dozen decades ago.

Whether it's a high-grade Parker, or a London Best built between the Wars, the dilemma remains, and with good reason. We can rationalize all we want about how the gun was made to be shot, that it's been doing it for years, that if something breaks there are folks who can fix it, and we can't control fate.

But none of that makes any difference when it's your favorite gun, because on the other side of the should-I-or-shouldn't-I coin are the arguments that the gun was made in a period when craftsmanship was valued above all else, and those craftsmen are no longer alive. It's probably irreplaceable if wrecked on the airlines, lost, stolen, or strayed, so even if it's insured, the money may not buy another. In the case of such guns as Purdeys or Hollands, where the companies are still functioning, a replacement can be built, but it's pretty certain that you didn't insure your gun for enough money to cover a new one being built. Let's face it—if you bought an old classic London Best for $10,000, you aren't going to insure it for the near-$60,000 replacement cost, if for no reason other than your insurance carrier probably won't allow it.

More and more, the really fine guns are staying closer to home, being used when the weather is just right and the trip is short by automobile, and there is no chance of anyone handling your gun except you. But what do we do when we book that long-awaited trip out of the country? Or the quail shoot down South? Or the annual Iowa pheasant extravaganza? There are airlines or motel rooms and baggage handlers, and there we are with The Big Problem again.

It's a shame, because many of these trips are the very ones where we would value the use of our best gun the most, yet even if we do, there's the gnawing uncertainty that things will come out fine in the end.

The sad part is, there are not many options open to us. We either take the gun, shoot it, and hope everything comes out okay, or we leave it at home in the safe, take a different gun, and don't enjoy the shooting as much, even if we enjoy the trip more.

I guess if you pushed me, I'd have to admit that I fall into the shoot them camp. The guns will likely outlive us, so what the hell. But I can certainly understand those who dread the $800 scratch in the stock. As I'll say repeatedly in this book, this is supposed to be fun, and if it's more fun to shoot the good guns, then we should do it. Like Gene Hill once said, if he owned an old Rolls Royce, he'd drive it. I probably would, too.

Thoughts on Chokes

CHOKE IS OFTEN A TOPIC where shotgunners gather, but my experience is that it is often seemingly more important to the intermediate-level shooter than either the beginner or the expert.

Don't get me wrong—choke is very important. But to the beginner it is complicated and foreign, and he would just as soon not deal with it. As he gains skill, he starts to understand the technical aspects of shooting, and choke becomes vital to him. His day is ruined if he goes, for example, to the dove field and finds that his modified and full double isn't the best prescription for the birds zipping by at 25 yards —he should have brought a skeet gun or at least remembered the other choke tubes.

Speaking of which, choke tubes have opened an entire new world to the obsessive-compulsives among our ranks who figure that the right choke or combination of chokes for the game, weather conditions, and the cover will never quite be within his grasp. He gets to mess with wrenches and tubes and choke-tube holders and generally fret a lot, which makes him the happiest.

When we buy a gun—used, factory, or custom—we naturally give a great deal of thought to what we will be using it for and how: the birds, the range we'll most likely shoot, the shot size, and so forth. A lot of things go into this choice, which is why our duck guns don't often resemble our woodcock guns. Choke is one of the factors, along with a whole host of other things that I hopefully have covered in this book.

But once the shooting starts, experienced wingshots of my acquaintance find that other things determine their success—the gun's fit, balance, and barrel length to name a few. Good shots come to rely less on pattern spread, and more on technique that ensures smooth gun handling and precise pointing.

Let's take pheasants for example. I like relatively tight chokes for pheasants because these big, tough birds require a big shot to anchor them, and tight chokes concentrate shot. The smaller the gauge, the tighter the choke. If I were to use a 20-gauge, my chokes would be modified and full; in a 16, I like a tight improved cylinder and improved modified; in a 12, I get by with a looser improved cylinder and modified. But there are some days when the birds will sit tight, and a skeet gun would do fine. If you find yourself in this situation, you can just wait the bird out a bit before shooting, allowing time for the pattern to open up.

In fact, this is one trait that marks the good shooters I've hunted with: the ability to wait for range to increase as the bird departs until pattern spread is optimal before they fire. Beginners feel that the expert shoots quickly and accurately, often dropping the bird before it has cleared the grass. In reality, the old smoothie waits them out, downing his birds at sure killing range without damaging the meat.

For most shooting, if we have to err, it is better to err on the side of being too tight. Nothing will ruin a shooting day as fast as not having enough gun, enough shot, or enough choke to adequately do the job. We end up crippling birds, the last thing we ever want to do.

Experienced shooters have, for a long time, had doubles bored with two, rather than one, gradient of choke between barrels. This adds incredible flexibility to the gun, especially when double triggers are employed. Following is the long explanation.

I recently got hold of a 16-gauge French guild gun, a plain but solid boxlock fired very little, through the good offices of a couple of friends who know I love these guns. They (the guns, not the friends) are every bit as well-made as Birmingham boxlocks from the same era at a fraction of the cost because they don't have the name recognition; the fact is, few of these guns that I've seen even have names. They were proofed at St. Etienne and are configured as boxlocks with 27½-inch barrels, 2½-inch chambers, straight grip/splinter forends, deep swamped ribs, and weighing 5½ pounds or thereabouts in 16-gauge, and 6¼ to 6½ in 12, plus or minus an ounce or two. The balance on each that I've encountered has been indistinguishable from Birmingham guns I own.

But what I really like about them is—I can actually shoot them. I don't mean I shoot them well; I don't/can't shoot anything well. I mean I can take them with me and not sweat bullets and blood that they might not get off the airliner when I do. We all know the concept of the "travel gun." This is a partial solution to the dilemma I talked about earlier in this section. My good friend, Mike McIntosh, even had one built to match his London Best so that he could travel and not worry that his net worth would be diminished at the end of a trip because his Wilkes didn't quite take the same route he did. Problem is, near as I can tell, Mac has started to like his travel gun so much—and its replacement cost is escalating fast enough—that now he sweats out whether that one makes it.

Obsessive-compulsive personality disorder aside, Mac has a point. A great gun deserves a great, albeit less expensive, stand-in. You want to shoot a pretty gun at a pretty bird, don't you? Now, the second-stringer has become as valuable, at least to you, as the star of the varsity. It'll make you crazy.

The downside that these guns offer is that the finish is usually poor, even though some of them have some rather good wood (others don't, of course), the length of pull is normally insanely short (many run 13½ inches, from what I've found), and the chokes are as tight as anything you'll see, normally being "demichoke and choke," which means at the pattern boards "tight and damn tight." Finally, the trigger pulls are almost uniformly too heavy, at least for my taste.

That's okay; everything can be fixed—stocks lengthened, bent if need be, refinished and, often as not, recheckered. Triggers can be lightened (my gunsmith tells me —when he takes my calls—that the triggers in these guns are all the same, straightforward and easy to work on), the barrels reblued if you want . . . and the chokes opened.

Starting with such tight chokes, I have been experimenting a bit, and with the 16-gauge I mention (the point of all this), I had the chokes of a tight modified and full opened to improved cylinder and improved modified.

I used the gun for the first time in Texas shooting quail, and the relatively tight left barrel came in handy more than once on birds that flushed wild in the ever-present Texas wind. Plains quail don't necessarily require a lot of shot, but they do often require a tighter choke. Although a heavier shot load will make a pattern more dense to a certain extent, you then have to contend with heavier recoil. I like the recoil and efficiency of 2½-inch shotshells, so I often use them on upland birds. But increasing their shot load dramatically is usually not an option. In the 2½-inch 16-gauge, the lightest ones are ⅞ ounce, and the heaviest only one ounce. So, if you want a more dense pattern, going to tighter chokes is really the only available option.

There are guns out there with chokes you'll only encounter as bespoke options, such as cylinder and full. Many guns built for driven birds, of course, have such wide variations between chokes, the drill being to fire the tight barrel first and the open barrel next because, unlike with our walked-up, going-away birds, the second shot is closer than the first. I have seen a couple of fine old English 12s in which the right barrel was bored full and the left barrel quarter choke; I can only assume that was the object here.

Of course, screw-in chokes have opened up an entire world of tinkering for just this sort of thing. IC/F, skeet/modified, F/F, IC/IC— any combination you want, with your choice of which barrel you want open, right or left, bottom or top. This is one of the great things about these chokes.

IC/F is a good combination for quail as well. The first shot on a covey rise is most often at IC range, but by the time we get around to picking out another bird, the range has often increased past where modified is effective. This is especially true if your gun of choice is a 20 (the traditional quail gun), and even more true if you fancy a 28.

Double Triggers and Auto Ejectors

I LIKE DOUBLE TRIGGERS. Aside from a couple of waterfowl guns, all of my guns have double triggers. I don't feel guns with double triggers are any more reliable, but they are certainly more flexible. But they could be even more useful to average shooters if we would just take advantage of them.

In most doubles—and here we're talking side-by-sides because double triggers on over-unders are pretty scarce—the front trigger fires the right barrel, which is the more open of the two chokes. The back or second trigger fires the left, tighter, barrel. There are exceptions, of course, and they can be found on any gun rack if you look hard enough. But a double made for a right-handed shooter will operate this way.

As I talked about at some length a bit ago, there is usually only one gradient of choke between the two barrels, as a standard—IC/M, M/F, for example. I like two gradients: IC/IM, C/M, etc. I feel the gun is more useful that way for my sort of shooting. You see this in guns often enough that if you want to try it out, you should have no trouble finding a combination you like for your shooting.

In typical American rough shooting behind dogs, the bird is almost always departing for parts unknown when the shooting starts. For this reason, of course, barrels are bored differently. The first shot is fired at a bird that is closer than it will be if and when you have to use the second barrel. Likewise on covey birds if you double—the second bird will be farther away than the first, everything being equal.

But as so often happens, a lone bird flushes at extreme range. The shooter lets it have the first, open barrel and follows up immediately with the second, tighter barrel. The first barrel may or may not do anything, but the second shot is the one that kills. The capability to fire the tight barrel first is the advantage I'm talking about. But to do it regularly, you have to think about it.

A couple of seasons ago, I was hunting Hungarian partridge with my friend, Ben Williams, near Livingston, Montana. The birds were wild, the coveys coming off the ground at 25 to 30 yards. By the time I picked out a bird, it was 40 yards off and intent on leaving the county. I was using a 12-gauge double bored IC/F. I hunted one whole day and shot six birds and never used the right barrel, instead firing the left barrel each time because of the extreme range. If I missed—as is my custom—I was out of business because the bird would be out of range for the IC barrel.

On shots where birds are coming toward you rather than going away, as with doves and waterfowl or driven shooting, if you get the chance to do it, it's easy to reverse the order and fire the tight barrel while the bird is still well out and then follow up with the open barrel as the bird gets closer. Most good shots I know handle driven birds in just such a manner.

You have to practice this until it becomes second nature. A sporting clays course is the place to try it out because of the variety of shots offered. The decision-making process entails an instant judgment of the target's range and then selection of the barrel that you feel will best handle that range. Then you shoot. It's really quite simple, and I've found that the process can actually make you a better shot because there is a consciousness involved, a thought process that helps calm the nerves.

Single-trigger guns, and most these days are single-selective, give you this advantage only in certain situations, such as the driven shooting I mentioned above, where there's a probability that all the shots will be pretty much alike. A barrel selector, even one combined with the safety so it's handy, is just too much to handle, at least for me. Maybe you think faster and can select the proper barrel when a bird goes up at the same time you're sliding off the safety, mounting, and swinging.

On the rare occasions I use single trigger guns in the uplands, I try to watch the dog; if she gets birdy at 40 yards, I'll slide the barrel selector to the tight barrel in case a bird goes up; if she gets interested in a piece of cover 25 yards away, I'll select the open barrel. If I'm hunting behind a pointing dog and he locks up at 60 yards, I choose the tight barrel, moving the selector to the open barrel when I get within 25 yards or so, right up until the bird flushes.

———————————

Automatic ejectors on a double are interesting items—interesting in the context of whether they are even necessary. I think that's a matter of personal taste. Like you, I grab spent hulls as they come out of the chambers. Shotgun shells can be a major source of litter (and they give away your best hunting spots) scattered upon the ground, the plastic eventually decomposing after a couple of million years. Maybe.

So is it any easier to catch ejected shells and stick them in your vest than it is to dig shells out with your fingers when they are lifted up by extractors? It is for me.

But do guns with ejectors cost more and can more go wrong with an ejector gun than with an extractor gun? Yes again. An extractor gun is also a tad lighter than an ejector gun, not always a good thing.

I've sort of hit a compromise here. Most of my upland guns have ejectors, while the doubles (side-by-sides) I use for waterfowl all have extractors. The need to quickly reload is more readily apparent in the uplands, where another bird or a straggler can get up right after we've emptied both barrels. In waterfowling, usually there are few surprise birds after the shooting starts. You also normally have time to reload and dispatch a cripple—although I confess that I most often use a pump (a Model 12)—because of the third shot, which I try to save for just that purpose.

I doubt that too many driven-bird shooters have tried it with extractors, and I also doubt that too many London guns are ordered without ejectors. The Southgate ejector has become about as standard as walnut for the stock. But if you are in the market for a gun (if?) and you're perusing the used gun ads or the used gun rack at a good retailer, don't necessarily turn up your nose at an extractor gun. True, most of them were not of the highest quality, but every once in awhile you'll run across one that will surprise you, like an extractor William Evans a friend of mine had built for waterfowling along the Platte River in Nebraska. He hates ejected shells slipping through his icy fingers and bouncing around the blind or floating in the water to spook the sharp-eyed Canadas, so he ordered the gun with extractors. It was a bit less expensive that way, which doesn't happen often—the option you want ending up cheaper.

Trigger Pulls and Flinching

I'M NOT SURE THAT THERE is anything that can more quickly make a good shot start to turn into a bad one than a faulty trigger. Specifically, faulty trigger pulls, and especially, heavy ones.

It seems to be a fact of shooting life that the longer you're at it, the lighter you like your triggers. Some competitive trap and skeet shooters like them so light as to be considered hair triggers and would be considered dangerous were they somewhere besides in the hands of experts under controlled conditions.

I'm not sure why this is so, but in some cases, I think it has to do with having shot a lot of shells. I think what happens is that the long-time shooter starts to subconsciously resist pulling the trigger—the forerunner of a flinch.

A true flinch is not waving the gun barrel around just before the shot or jerking spasmodically in anticipation of recoil. Rather, a flinch occurs when the shooter just can't make himself pull the trigger. The first few times, he thinks it's the gun, because he's sure he did his part. But what happens is the finger doesn't pull, it sort of twitches, not hard enough to make the gun go off, but enough that the shooter has the subliminal recollection that he did, indeed, pull the trigger.

Recoil has a cumulative effect—it adds up over the years. A flinch is a response formulated by the body to keep from getting hammered by recoil one more time. The problem is that you don't know you're doing it until it happens. One time you're fine, the next time. . .

There are ways to try to fool a flinch. A long layoff is one, although not very acceptable. Since target shooters suffer more often from flinches than do game shots, I suppose swearing off trap, skeet, and sporting clays for a while is probably a good idea. Some target shots who have the flinches and don't want to quit their games find some relief in the form of release triggers, which fire when the trigger is released rather than pulled. Another way around things, since recoil is the culprit, is to shoot heavier guns, smaller gauges, or guns with recoil reducers in the stock. Longer barrels have less muzzle blast, so they are a good idea, and hearing protection goes a long way toward making a gun feel like it kicks less. Sometimes just adding a recoil pad to a checkered or hard plastic butt does the trick. Naturally, if the stock fit is wrong so that you get whacked upside your head every time you shoot, you'll get a flinch in a hurry. Like maybe the second shot.

After one especially active trip to Mexico for white-winged doves, I came home in time for the grouse opener in September. I found I had the beginnings of a flinch. I'd been shooting with poor—or no—ear protection (like a knucklehead), and I had used a five-pound, 28-gauge with 26-inch barrels, spiteful recoil, and dreadful muzzle blast. There were a lot of doves that year, and I had taken my share of shots over a full week's shoot. So when I got back and started grouse hunting—using that same gun—it didn't come as much of a surprise that the gun didn't shoot when I pulled the trigger. A switch to a heavier, longer-barreled 16-gauge took care of the problem, but it could have been much worse; in this case, my almost-flinch was tied to only one gun.

One thing that helps when we reach the point where recoil becomes a problem is light triggers. Light triggers, of course, allow the gun to go off with less pressure, so very often it seems to fire itself. I don't mean that they are unsafe; instead, light triggers allow the gun to be discharged at the very instant that the sight picture seems to look right.

Back in the old days, I drove sports cars a lot—rallies, club races, that sort of thing. What I always appreciated about a car that was set up correctly was the way I could almost think it through a curve or turn; the car seemed to be able to read my mind, sensing as if it were alive what I wanted it to do and when, and then doing it without conscious effort on my part. That's how it is with a gun whose triggers are set correctly light; the gun itself seems to sense when everything is right and then fires as an extension of your will.

The shotgun swing, like the golf swing, the tennis swing, the baseball swing, is a gross motor-muscle movement, a full range of motion, only a small portion of which holds the action for which the swing exists—there is only a brief instant during the entire swing when the golf ball, the tennis ball, or the baseball are actually struck. The timing of the huge swings of a David Justice, a Michael Chang, or a Greg Norman exist and are perfectly timed so that everything comes together the way they intend for a nanosecond when the bat, the racquet, and the club make contact with the ball. Their swings all establish momentum and power, bring their hand-held tool to the proper plane, and follow through so that the motion remains smooth throughout. Somewhere in that entire motion, contact is made almost incidentally.

The shotgun swing, similarly, is intended to track a target on the proper plane, establish the right amount of forward allowance, to make "contact"—that is, to fire the gun—and to follow through. Only briefly somewhere in that motion is the shot—the reason for the swing—triggered. That's why light triggers help: They allow the shot to be triggered as part of a fluid, graceful, motion. If a gun's trigger pulls are heavy, there is by necessity a hesitation that will, ever so slightly, interrupt the swing and rob it of the fluid motion it requires to be successful from shot to shot. That is also why light triggers help those who have shot a carload of shells; their swings are so finely tuned that the interruption caused by heavy triggers is fatal to good shooting. And if you have the makings of a flinch, light triggers allow the gun to go off with the slightest, almost imperceptible, effort.

What are light triggers? In terms of weight, it was established by gun-makers long ago that trigger pulls are at their best when the first barrel (on a double-trigger gun) lets off at half the weight of the gun, and the second lets go at up to 25 percent more. On a six-pound gun, this means three pounds and 3½ to 3¾.

The second trigger on such a gun is not pulled back, as is the first trigger, but instead is pulled up. The shooter's hand finds this pull easier, so trigger weights such as those above feel the same to his hand. The heavier the gun, the heavier the pulls that can be adjusted into the gun without their feeling heavy; a four-pound trigger on an eight-pound gun feels like a three-pound pull on a six-pound gun. A single trigger on a double, of course, needs to have both mechanisms set up the same—half the weight of the gun—because the hand remains in the same position for both shots.

Triggers should have no creep at all, but rather they should let off like what someone once described as "glass breaking." When the pressure threshold is reached to fire a gun, the hammer should just let go—no slack to be taken up first, no matter how light the pull. A gunsmith can adjust the trigger pulls for you on any gun, boxlock or sidelock, for a fee. Usually, it isn't cheap. I have paid from $50 to $90 per trigger for adjustments.

One of the selling points of sidelock guns has long been that they can be adjusted to give "perfect" trigger pulls to a customer's specifications. In reality, a good gunsmith can adjust boxlock triggers to give the same level of performance. I shoot both styles of guns, and if the triggers are proper for a gun's weight, I can't tell any difference. Some gunsmiths do not work on triggers, so you may have to shop around to find one who does.

Triggers have a tendency to get heavier with time. One sidelock 20 that I shoot often for quail had its triggers adjusted when I got the gun several years ago, and I shot it pretty well (for me). Then I started missing, so I put a trigger-pull gauge on it, and the pulls had become heavier by about a half-pound each trigger. It went back to the shop.

If you own a fine gun by a maker still in business, they will often ask that you send the gun to them every year at the end of the season for cleaning and inspection, and in many places, such as England, it's a tradition to do so. The maker will look for worn/broken parts, will clean the locks, and will test the pulls to make sure they meet the specifications you've given him.

For most of us, that's impractical and expensive; we send the gun off when it breaks—that's our tradition. If you get a trigger-pull gauge, you can easily keep track of the pulls on all your guns. Don't trust your memory about how the pulls felt when they were right; at our age, we know what memory can be like. Get a gauge or take it to a gunsmith who has one and find out for sure. Very often, it's just a case of the triggers needing a good cleaning every few years, depending on how much you shoot.

Starting Kids

NOT TOO LONG AGO, I WAS pestering my daughter, Amy, and son-in-law, Steve, about when they were going to start giving me grandkids. I used the usual little ploy, hinting broadly that Steve may not be a fully functioning model.

Amy accused me of wanting to have a grandson so I could teach him how to do some of the things I do well—swear and drink Scotch. I was surprised, because she said it like those were bad things.

Anyhow, this got me off on a tangent, so I started rummaging through the gun cabinet for a shotgun that would be about right for a first-time shooter, boy or girl. I came across the one I started both my sons on. Amy started hunting later, as a (childless) adult.

It was a single-barrel 20-gauge with improved modified choke and a hammer. Probably about what you and I started on. The 20 is a good choice because you can load it down for light recoil and still have an effective shotgun at close range (the .410 is not a kid's/learner's gun). The IM choke gives a young shooter a chance at longer ranges. You have to consider that by the time they get over being startled by the flush and get into action, they're going to be a tad slow. The tighter choke still gives them a chance at 35 to 40 yards. The single shot, of course, is for safety.

But I don't like the hammer, and the balance on guns such as this is, frankly, pathetic. Remington, among others, makes some nice youth-model shotguns in pump and autoloading design that are much better for starting a kid. If you're worried about a repeating gun and the safety factor, just give him or her one shell at a time.

I started the guys off by having them shoot toy balloons blowing across a plowed farm field. When they missed, the puff of dirt from the pattern showed them where. The balloons break in a most satisfying manner, and if the wind is more than 10 mph, the target can get tricky and out of range in a hurry.

From there, we started shooting clays at the gun club. Station 7 outgoing (low house). Then station 7 incomers, where a little lead and swing is needed or you'll shoot behind.

Then we shot some from a Trius trap, varying the angles—high floaters to start with, then low birds that were fairly well humming. Finally, we went back to the club and shot trap standing right behind the trap house. The ranges are short compared with the 16-yard mark, but you had to be ready and fairly quick, and the oscillating trap varied the angle so that they couldn't groove in. This shot also convincingly mimics how a bird comes out from in front of a pointing dog—good practice.

The next step, after the required hunter's safety class and license, was a shooting preserve, a club I belonged to at the time that would more or less leave you alone, providing you with a bird field and solitude. I had good dogs, and if I need a guide to find birds in a preserve's 40-acre field, I'd better think up a different hobby.

There, under carefully controlled situations—my setter on a staunch point and Dear Old Dad close at hand—they started shooting birds. I guess I sort of got carried away, because they shot a lot of birds, according to the bills the club sent me. But the good thing that happened was that this repeated exposure to birds did the same thing that batting practice does if you're a ballplayer: It builds muscle memory and allows you to get the jitters and eagerness under control. The transition to wild birds was just the natural next step.

For the sake of our sport's future, it is up to us to take a youngster aside—doesn't have even have to be a blood relative—and teach him or her the ways of birds and guns and the sporting life.

Matter of fact, each year, more women join the ranks of those who shoot; they comprise the largest growth segment of our sport. Over the next couple of years, you're going to see a lot of products and equipment aimed specifically at this market by the larger purveyors. In my home state of Michigan, which sells the greatest number of hunting licenses in the country, from 25 percent to 50 percent of the enrollees in the state-mandated Hunter Safety program are girls and women seeking their first hunting license. There could be no better indicator of the health of our sport.

So if it's a son, a daughter, or wife, get them interested in the shooting sports. It's our future.

By the way, six months ago, Sarah Virginia, my granddaughter, checked in. When she's 10 or 11, I'll help her dad and mom teach her to shoot. The Scotch will have to wait a bit.

Tips

A GOOD LONDON OIL FINISH can easily be brought back to life with some linseed oil rubbed into the stock by hand. A hard, shiny polyurethane finish, once damaged, must be stripped off and reapplied. So while an oil finish is expensive and time-consuming to apply, it lasts, much like the gun itself.

More and more shooters are realizing the benefits of longer (27½-inch to 28-inch) barrels that are thin and finely tapered. Many of the short barrels (25-inch to 26-inch) are thick-walled and heavy. This heaviness detracts from the supposed "speed" for which short barrels are known. Next time you're in the market for a shotgun (and aren't we always?), look the gun over carefully at the muzzles.

Fine guns are much more likely to be worn by opening and closing than by shooting. Never slam a double closed. Instead, hold the release lever far right, raise stock to barrels, and ease the lever to its closed position. All lugs are then seated, but without the force that will produce wear. A fine gun so treated and properly lubricated will last quite a number of lifetimes.

If you get enough phone books each year to last five, put some of your old ones to good use—spend a little time at the patterning board checking the penetration of various loads by shooting into the books. Penetration is easy to check by opening the book to the last page where penetration ceases, noting the page number, and comparing the number with subsequent shots at different books. One thing we know you'll find out: The more expensive loads with harder (high antimony content) shot will give not only better patterns but the best penetration as well.

When traveling by air with a fine gun, experienced wingshooters find that a gun carried in a takedown hard case is much less likely to be opened for inspection at the airport than a full-length hard case.

Buying a New Used Gun

SINCE WE'RE ALWAYS TALKING about or thinking about or scheming for a new gun —even if it's a used one—we may as well spend a little time talking about what to look for.

The gun-trading business is a funny one, one of the last places where *caveat emptor* applies, and unless you know what you want, you might as well take your money, make a nice little pile out of it, light it, and toast marshmallows—at least you'd get some value out of it.

I'm not implying that gun dealers are dishonest—most are not. They won't knowingly sell you something dangerous that could harm you; everybody knows a lawyer these days, so it's not worth it.

But the guns we often see are overpriced given their condition and what it will take in terms of cash to make them right—and I don't mean right for you; I talk about that in another chapter. I mean what it will take to make the gun mechanically right enough to shoot and be sure it will last. The best bet, of course, is to buy a reliable name that is in good condition. "Good," naturally, is the operative word.

———————

Let's say that you have arrived at Uncle Friendly's Gun Shoppe and Furnace Repair, and you spot an old American classic in the rack. It's the gauge you like best, so you wander over and pluck it down—or ask to see it if Unk doesn't like the customers pawing the goods on their own.

The first thing that should come to your attention is the overall condition of the gun: the wood and steel. If the steel is without blueing, that doesn't mean much. But if the exterior of the barrels are pitted or, worse yet, dinged or dented, and the wood is without finish and cracked, splintered, or shows careless use, put the gun back.

An analogy here is in order: If you were to look at a used car, and it was dirty, rusty, the seats were torn, the fenders flapping in the wind, and the windshield cracked, you would probably not believe the seller when he told you that even though it was rough looking on the outside, the engine, transmission, brakes, and electrical system had been immaculately maintained. You would, justifiably, feel that someone misused the car, and they probably misused it in every way possible, the smart money deducing that the guy who doesn't pick the orange peels up off the floor in the back seat also probably doesn't get the oil changed every 3,000 miles.

Likewise, a beat-up exterior of a shotgun showing not just hard use but misuse should tell you all you need to know about how the gun will function mechanically—you shouldn't even have to look. It doesn't matter what Unk is charging for the gun, you work too hard for your money to waste it on a gun that's shot out.

Guns have lifespans, and those lifespans can be measured in years and in rounds fired. After a certain time, which varies from gun to gun even by the same maker, they are just old and tired. What you are looking for are signs of age—like the car (and you and me), it isn't always the years; sometimes it's the mileage. A competitive shooter's trap gun may have had a quarter of a million shells through it in a few short years; an original Parker VHE has not fired a shot in 30 years, but those years were spent in the back of a barn right next to where they stored the humid hay—one of these is high mileage, the other is too much time.

Generally, if well-maintained, a fine gun by a good maker has a virtually unlimited lifespan. There are guns out there in the pheasant fields on their third sets of barrels; every spring has been replaced, some several times; they have been put back on face when needed; the stocks have been refinished a half-dozen times—maybe it's a brand new stock.

Look, how long would your present vehicle last you if you made the commitment to replace every part when it broke or became worn, and I don't mean just tires and sparkplugs? I mean the steering wheel and a rusty fender and pitted bumper and a stained dashboard and the seats when the springs start to sag. You could make the car stay like new forever, theoretically. In practice, we don't do that because it's cheaper to simply buy a new vehicle. Plus, we get tired of it. But those who collect and restore classic cars know that, for a price, they can roll out a 1956 Chevy that's better than the day it was made. (For those of you who are about my age, "1956 Chevy" should bring back some memories. . .)

Well, the same can be done with a gun. What you want to do is buy one that has been maintained this way—no different than wanting to buy a used car from someone who was obsessive-compulsive about his vehicles. You just have to know how to look. And the overall condition is the best place to start.

Okay, so bad overall condition at first glance probably means bad news, but if the first glance doesn't make you turn away, that doesn't necessarily mean much. Just as we all know people who wax their cars every month but forget to change the oil, there are those who keep the outside of their guns looking great and forget to lubricate the hinge pin. So, you must look deeper. Here, the grade of the gun comes into play.

A fine gun costs a lot of money and, adjusted for time, it always has. It is a fact of human nature that most people take better care of things for which they paid a lot of money than they do cheap things, so the odds are that a fine, expensive, gun was better maintained, on average, than a cheap gun. Not always, but often enough that you can give it some credence. So, a used Purdey is probably going to be in better overall shape than a used Parker Trojan of the same vintage. Take this into consideration as well.

Now that you have the gun in hand, the exterior is okay, so you look closer. Start with the top lever. If it is offset well to the left, the gun has been opened and closed—hard—a number of times, say several zillion. This means wear. Doubles are not made to be slammed shut, but they are by the unknowing. Fine guns normally don't shoot loose; instead they are worn loose, and most of the wear comes from opening and closing them with too much gusto too often.

Improper cleaning—or no cleaning at all—also leads to problems. Particles of partially fired powder are harder than gun steel. If this residue is left on the gun, each time it is fired, recoil causes this grit to be ground into the steel, usually at critical junctures where the fit, of necessity, is tight. This loosens the gun further.

How can you detect this? Well, you can look for pitting around the axis where the standing breech meets the water table, and you can look to see if the gun is off face; that is, it doesn't bolt securely. I pluck a hair from my thinning locks and shut it in the action at the top, near the rib. A tight gun should securely hold the hair in place—maybe even snip it off neatly. If you close the action and can pull the hair out, it's possible that the gun is off face.

With the gun closed in your hands, remove the forend and wiggle the stock and barrels laterally against one other. There should be no play. If it wiggles perceptibly, it's loose.

Now, let's examine the barrels. Look down the tubes, first one, then the other. There should be no pitting. If they look smooth, ask to use a cleaning rod and shove a cloth or tissue down the barrels. Unscrupulous gun dealers have been known to disguise pitting with talcum powder, which fills in the holes. The cleaning rod should remove it and give you a better look at the bores.

If they appear to be okay, look down the barrels again, this time make sure it's toward a bright light. The rings you see should be concentric; if they look oblong, there's a chance the barrels are bent. Avoid this gun also. If the rings look fine, take the barrels, sans forend, dangle them from your index finger by the hook, and snap the barrels up and down their length with a fingernail of your other hand. They should ring like church bells. If you hear a dull thud at any spot, this indicates rust under either the top or bottom rib. Keep shopping.

Trigger pulls are vital, so carry some snap caps and test the gun. There should be little or no creep, and the pulls should be light but not overly so, which can indicate worn sears. I like to put pressure on the triggers with the safety on, let up, then release the safety. If the sears are badly worn, the hammers may fall when you do this. No good.

Look at the muzzles. If the outsides of the barrels are not touching one another in the center, there's a good chance they have been lopped off. Also, if they are an odd measurement, it may indicate that they have been cut. That tip is most reliable with American guns. Makers of these manufactured their barrels in even-number lengths —28 inches, 26 inches, and so forth. Continental makers most often used centimeters, of course, and bespoke guns from any nation could have been any length that suited the fancy of the original owner.

A choke gauge may or may not give an indication of the choke and thus the patterns the gun will shoot, but, again, it's not reliable. I have a classic Birmingham boxlock 16-gauge that the choke gauge says is Cylinder and Full, yet it throws the prettiest Improved Cylinder and Improved Modified patterns you ever saw. Suffice it to say that there is more to the choke and the resulting pattern in a shotgun barrel than the size of the hole in the end.

While you have the snap caps handy, load them into the chambers, shut the gun, point the muzzles at the ceiling, and shake it up and down. You should not be able to hear the dummy cartridges jiggle. If you can, this means that upon firing live shells, there will be a tiny fraction of an inch in which the shell can get a running start, under recoil, and slam into the standing breech. If this hasn't loosened the action yet, it will. And it's expensive to fix. Plus it makes the gun kick like hell.

With snap caps still loaded, it's time to try the ejectors. They should throw the caps an equal distance and should leave the gun at the same time. Very often, the right barrel's ejector will be weaker due to use. If the gun has extractors, make sure these lift the shells out far enough that you can get hold of them easily; if they don't, the extractor rod is probably worn.

I think it's imperative to carry with you a chamber-length gauge to ascertain that critical measurement. Any foreign-made gun can potentially have short chambers, and the dealer may well be unaware of it. Some gauges—notably the 16—from classic American makers often had short chambers, too. If you can get short shells in the gauge you want—and they're readily available these days—this shouldn't make too much difference. I vote against having chambers lengthened; the gun was made to handle a certain load, and extending chambers could make it tempting to shoot shells too hot for the gun.

There are additional ways of ascertaining if a gun has life left in it, but these are the basics and should serve you well. The cosmetics can be cleaned up—a lot of it, such as stock refinishing, are enjoyable projects for you to tackle yourself.

But I'm willing to bet you can't replace a worn trigger sear or weak hammer spring any better than I can.

So now let's say you've found a nice old shooter, one in good mechanical condition. Let's look at the things you can do to make it yours. The most important part of the gun, for the sake of good shooting, is the stock, specifically, its fit. Stock-fit problems come about because the wood is either too short or too long, too much or not enough cast if you like cast, too high or low at the comb, all of which can be fixed. Stocks can be bent up or down, in or out, lengthened with a recoil pad or a chunk of matching wood, shortened via a bandsaw. All of this can be done at the hands of a competent stockmaker—not necessarily your local gunsmith.

The critical measurements are drop at comb and heel. You must know your measurements, either through a good fitting or through experience—experience being the better of the two. If the stock is too high for you, you may consider taking it down yourself—a fun winter project. Shoot the gun periodically to make sure you're not taking off too much wood, and when it hits where you point it when you snap it up and shoot without aiming, refinish it. Try to shoot as you would in the field, with your face firmly but comfortably on the stock but not mashed into it. Cheeking too deeply and accepting what you get as gospel results in one type of fit when you're shooting patterns, but a different type of fit when you're shooting birds, when we all have a tendency to lift our faces a bit so we can see.

This is where you may give some thought to where you want the pattern to strike. I cover this later in a piece titled "Bird Fit," but we can say right now that most upland guns shoot best when they place the bulk of their pattern slightly above the point of aim (actually, the point of point). This is because upland birds are normally rising, and the high-shooting gun allows you to keep the bird in view and still hit. If the stock is pretty good but shoots just a tad too high, consider putting a larger front bead on it. We don't use the bead to aim, but we do have a subliminal tendency to point with the highest thing at the end of the barrel; a big bead makes us subconsciously hold a bit lower. Speaking of shooting high, remember that a thick comb will shoot a bit higher than a gun with a thin comb, all other dimensions being equal.

If the stock on the gun you choose has a pistol grip or a semipistol and you want a straight grip, a good wood man can do that for you and rechecker the results. The reverse, of course, is not true, and if you want a pistol grip and the gun does not have one, you're stuck unless you have a new stock made.

Actually, the solution is to have a new stock made if there are too many things about a stock that are wrong. Let's say the gun you're customizing has a stock that's too short, has too much drop at comb and heel, and has a pistol grip and you prefer a slim Prince-of-Wales grip. You're talking about lengthening, bending, changing the pitch, changing the grip, and recheckering. For the time and money you'll spend, you're probably better off having a new stock made.

That's pretty much the wood; now let's look at the steel. Although you can have gun barrels shortened, I don't suggest it. The point of impact is often changed for one barrel or the other, and you'll have little if any choke left. And you can't lengthen the existing barrels, of course. But you can change the chokes, the easiest way being to loosen them. (They are almost impossible to tighten unless you have screw-in chokes installed, which only works with barrels that are not too worn at the muzzles.)

Here is where you may want to consider some different choke combinations. Instead of the traditional IC/M or M/F, you may want to go with something like IC/F or IC/IM or cylinder (skeet) and improved cylinder, depending upon what you plan to use the gun for. For this reason, if you run across a good deal on a mechanically fine shotgun with M/F chokes, that's good—your options are wide open.

Trigger pulls are usually a problem in used guns. They have a tendency to grow heavier with time and use, and a good cleaning alone may solve the problem. If not, then a good trigger 'smith can do the job for around $50 to $75 per trigger. At the same time, worn sears and springs can be replaced (although with older guns and most of those from Europe, he'll have to make and properly harden the parts from scratch, which can get pricey).

Engraving on the action can be re-cut, case color hardening brought back to life, and slight dings and scratches in the barrels can be fixed. Even minor bore pitting can be lapped out.

Finally, a nice blueing (blacking) job sets off the whole gun quite nicely. Now, you have your own heirloom, one you essentially made for yourself.

Nontoxic Shot

I GLANCED AT MY WATCH AS the flock of mixed snows and blues wheeled low over the pounding surf of Hudson Bay and headed inland, their eyes locked on our rag and silhouette decoys deployed in what we liked to think was an enticing pattern in front of and around our blind. It was clear that shooting time would arrive before the birds did.

Heh heh heh.

The flock of about two dozen set their wings and coasted down the invisible hill that is their landing pattern. When they were back-pedaling above our set, choosing the spot they wanted to land, we stood, the three of us, and picked out our birds.

Wham! Chris's pure white snow slumped and went slack, frozen in death 20 yards above the tundra.

Pow! Jake's huge blue goose's neck snapped back before it started its plummet toward earth.

Because I'm older, less intense, and slower, I shot last, catching a white bird at 45 yards as it clawed for elevation, intent upon being anywhere but right there. Hammered, the bird fell in a satisfying arc and bounced when it hit the ground.

According to everything I have been able to find out, these were the first legal wild North American waterfowl to be taken with bismuth shot—in the first minute of the first day of the first season in the first country on the continent to allow the use of the then-new, non-toxic loads.

Bismuth Shot

Bismuth shot—a bismuth/tin alloy, actually—has become another choice for waterfowlers after steel (iron, actually) shot. It was September 1, 1993, the first day of Manitoba's waterfowl season. Canada had legalized the new load for use in that country, and we had gone to Hudson Bay to shoot snows with it.

And snows we shot. In an hour and a quarter, our combined limit of 15 birds lay on the ground behind the blind. The rest of the week, we tested the shells, took photos, shot a few birds each day, hunted ptarmigan (but not with bismuth), and generally enjoyed being a hundred air miles from nowhere and north of the fifty-fifth parallel.

Since the advent of steel shot, hunters have hoped for, and manufacturers have searched for, an alternative to steel. Steel will bulge your gun barrel, rumor had it; steel would score the barrels of a fine gun, they said; steel didn't hit as hard as lead—it was daisy petals and fingernail clippings, they said.

Well, yes and no. I'm a supporter of steel shot, for all the reasons the U.S. Fish and Wildlife Service trotted out for public inspection, mainly death to waterfowl by lead shot ingestion. That has not necessarily made me very popular at times, but hell, if it wasn't that, it would be something else.

Anyway, it is not for fine old guns, especially fine old doubles. It does not hit as hard as lead nor kill as far. But it will kill, and it probably won't bulge your barrel, provided the barrel is no tighter than modified.

The biggest problem with steel is when we try to compare it with lead (and every year, there are fewer of us out there freezing our keesters off who remember what it was like to shoot ducks with lead). The comparison doesn't hold up. You have to shoot bigger sizes—the shotshell manufacturers recommend going up a full size (from 4s to 2s, for example). You also have to stay conservative in the ranges at which you shoot your birds. Instead of shooting at 45 yards with lead, shoot at 35 with steel. Or, more to the point for too many waterfowlers, instead of flaring the birds by shooting at them at 65 yards with lead, flare them at 55 with steel. My experience has been that the folks doing the most grumbling about the short killing range of steel will shoot at birds out of range no matter what they're using—they crippled birds with lead, too, for the same reason; they've just chosen to forget that part. If you read some of the older literature, circa 1940, you'll see writers decrying skybusting and long-range crippling by waterfowlers—and they were, of course, using lead.

Along comes bismuth shot and tungsten, too, the newest addition to the nontoxic field, although I hope not the last. Bismuth hits harder downrange because it's heavier and retains velocity better than steel. It is malleable so it won't harm barrels, even those on fine old guns. It kills, and kills effectively, although I suggest you shoot a size between lead and steel (lead 4s = bismuth 2s = steel BBs). Tungsten, relatively new, is as hard as steel and hits with more force than either bismuth or steel. Both of these are very expensive. You may want to use them only in special circumstances. If I were going on a field hunt for Canada geese and the limit were two, I'd use bismuth or tungsten. If I'm hunting streaking bluebills on big water in the wind and the limit's five, it's got to be steel —I'll just shoot too many times. And if I shoot behind a crossing bird— and I will—it doesn't matter to either me or the duck if I'm shooting steel, bismuth, tungsten, or an ounce and a quarter of lapel pins.

To be a better shooter, a more clever collector of waterfowl, the answer lies not in our chambers, but in ourselves. It isn't about loads, it's about decoy placement. Feet-per-second doesn't matter as much as calling and holding still. The difference between 2s and BBs isn't as important in terms of birds in the bag as the difference between a trained and an untrained retriever.

As I mention in another place in this book, those who have never shot lead at ducks and geese don't know what they're missing, so they happily go along shooting ducks at 30 yards, placing their blinds where the birds want to be, and calling at the right pitch, the right cadence, the right time, and the right amount.

We are asking our shot load to make us better hunters. It can't; it can only make us better shooters, and there's a difference.

Bird Fit

GOOD GUN FIT, WHICH I HAVE emphasized as being of paramount importance for good shooting, is like class: hard to define, but you probably know it when you see it, and you certainly know when it's missing.

But "good" conjures up the question, "Good for what?" I hope that I have not given the impression that one fit works for everything, because it doesn't. At least not as well as it could. Now maybe some (most) stock fitters out there will disagree with me, but—in keeping with our belief that shotguns are specialty items—a driven-pheasant gun you'd haul with you to Scotland might not have the same stock configuration as a gun intended for, say, ruffed grouse in Vermont.

Let me give you an example: the driven birds I mentioned. English stock fitters who fit for that sport like long, straight stocks with minimal drop at comb and heel. They feel that such a stock does a number of things. First, it reduces felt recoil because it minimizes the stock's upward jump into your face when you fire. And since driven-bird shooters normally shoot a lot, this is important.

Next, a high stock allows for a little built-in lead for birds that are coming at you. This allows you to see the bird up until the final instant when you cover it and fire. Finally, a long stock moves the gun's weight forward a bit, making it smoother for long swings. Mounting a long stock is not usually a problem, because with driven birds, you can see them well ahead of time, normally, and can get ready to mount. Such a stock is also fine for plains or open-country shooting for many of the same reasons: You have time to mount, and the birds in this case (especially pheasants), though not incoming, are rising flushers, requiring a little assistance from some built-in lead.

Finally, and I really think they're on to something here, British stock fitters feel that a long stock pulls the shooter "into the gun," making it less likely he'll raise his face to get a peek, one of the chief causes of missing.

Now, take an opposite situation: brush shooting for such birds as ruffed grouse and woodcock. Here, I like a stock that is shorter and with a bit more drop, because I often don't get my face down where it should be in the time I have to shoot before the bird is gone. I like a stock that will pattern about 55/45 above the point of aim, compared with the 60/40 I like for an open-country shotgun's pattern. This pattern allows for all those varying angles these birds can throw at you. Since the mounting borders right on the edge of frenzy in grouse covers, a shorter stock causes fewer hang-ups on your clothing.

For bobwhites, I like a short stock because of quick mounts, although I'm not talking about the kind where I'll bang my nose with my thumb under recoil. I like a flat-shooting gun (about like the grouse gun), because most quail shots are at eye level or slightly above and the birds are usually going straight away or at slight angles. Here, shooting over the top of a departing bird is a real possibility.

Simply put, with an open-country gun, I see a lot of rib; on a grouse gun a bit less, and on a quail gun a bit less than that. This may or may not be true for you, and if you do great with one gun or one fit, you have simplified your shooting life in a way I can only envy. There is a lot of truth in the old adage, "Beware the man with only one gun." But what fun is that?

Gun Case Etcetera

SOME OF THE NIFTIEST STUFF for shooting includes the array of great little items designed to go in our gun cases for cleaning and protecting a fine gun. I'm talking about things like oil bottles and two-piece rosewood cleaning rods and snap caps and all the assortment of neat things designed to make you feel like a real sport and to dress up your gun collection.

Many of them have no value to most of us. Others are very useful, and you should have them for your guns, no matter their grade or configuration. For example, I can think of nothing, to me, more useless than a striker box. Unlike some of my American gun-writing colleagues, I use American terms. I use "gauge" rather than "bore," "firing pin" instead of "striker," "screw" instead of "pin" (you can see where the confusion comes—to a Brit, a firing pin would be a firing screw, of which there aren't any). But I vary on occasion. The term "turnscrews" instead of "screwdrivers" just seems so much more correct because it refers, to me, only to a set of ground-to-fit tools made for your gun, with the handles coming from the same blank of wood that forms your stock and forend. Perfect. (An aside: Why are they not called "turnpins"?)

Back to the striker box, a little round box made from various materials (nickel, rosewood, horn, et al) that fits in your VC case and holds extra firing pins and springs. Now really, can any of us replace a broken firing pin in the field using only our incredible skill and the proper turnscrew with the matching Turkish walnut handle? Well, I can't. On the other hand, well-made snap caps are a must. These dummy shot-shells cushion the firing pin so you can dry-fire your gun to drop the hammers prior to long storage or to test the trigger pulls for weight and creep.

Muzzle-stoppers, which you don't see often, are great. They keep dust and grit out of a gun's barrels when it's stored in an upright position (which it really shouldn't be for long; oil from the action will work its way downward into the wood and eventually rot it). Stoppers—once called "tompons," a term now little used and, for the life of me, I can't understand why—can also give thin muzzles in fine guns some small measure of protection when the gun is carried assembled in a full-length soft case, or gunslip.

But on the other hand, nickel or gold-plated oil and solvent bottles are now remnants of the past; modern gun oils and solvents are so much easier to use in sprays or from easy-applicating cans than an oil bottle with its little metal dipper-type dispenser. And the cartridge extractor is also a dinosaur, a throwback to the days of lousy ammunition and brass cases that would rupture and expand and had to be dug out in the field.

Most of the other stuff, however, has good uses today. A brass chamber brush is used to clean, of course, the chambers of your gun; a trigger-pull gauge tells you at what weight your gun's triggers are letting off, thus alerting you when it's time for a trip to the gunsmith; one of those little rubber, trigger-guard bumpers keeps your middle finger from getting bruised upon recoil if your grip isn't quite right. Then there's the gauge that checks chamber length on older guns so that you don't shoot long shells in short chambers—an experience that does neither you nor the gun any good. The choke gauge gives you at least an approximation of choke in a shotgun's barrel by measuring the inside diameter of the muzzle—although much more goes into regulating the pattern thrown by a barrel's choke than the hole's size at the end.

Finally, there's the handguard, a leather-covered steel gadget that keeps your forend hand away from hot barrels on splinter-forend guns. In truth, shooting gloves are better. Once, while in Mexico shooting whitewings, I fried a handguard to the barrels. When I finally got the thing off the gun, it took the blueing with it. Some gunsmiths say that the chemicals used to tan the leather in a handguard will dull or even remove the barrels' finish as well. Maybe, maybe not. But like the rest of this stuff, a handguard sure looks nice in your gun case.

Ordering a Custom Gun

THE TIME WILL COME, eventually, when the urge will hit you as overpowering as anything you've felt since puberty reared its ugly head, lo these many years ago—the need to order a custom gun.

This urge usually comes about after a rather predictable evolution in your shooting/gun-buying habits. First step, of course, comes as a beginner when you buy something off the rack and start shooting with it. As you get better, you realize that there are ways a gun can be tweaked to be better for you—maybe the stock is lengthened or shortened or the chokes opened, for example. Nothing major, certainly nothing expensive. Both of those will follow.

Then, you spot a gun that's just what you "need," that being the operative word throughout this entire procedure. Maybe it's a side-by-side double instead of an over-under or an over-under instead of an autoloader—doesn't matter. In any event, in your mind, it represents a step upward in the evolutionary chain of events. This gun will be the right action, the right barrel length, and the right weight, but the rest of the configuration, in your mind, needs some work. So, it becomes a "project gun," and you sink a lot of cash into making it right: Perhaps the chokes are opened. The stock configuration is changed to fit you (because by now you've become aware of your true measurements), and you decide to have it bent. Maybe you have the pistol grip removed and the stock made into a straight grip.

By the time you get all of this done, the gun is right for you, and you may end up merrily shooting this one forever, and if so, good for you and I doff my hat to you as a better man than I see staring back at me each morning in the mirror. But most likely, this only lasts for a while, and you start another project gun, this one more expensive and the work more extensive. And then another. And another.

Time goes along, as it has a bad habit of doing, and you are likely to find yourself gravitating toward a certain, well-defined type of shotgun—sidelock side-by-sides from England or the Continent,

Italian over-unders, or maybe classic old Ansley Foxes or Parkers or Smiths. Whatever. Time will make you pretty sure what you want, and you spend money tearing around trying to find the one gun that's just so. The odds are, if you keep at it long enough, you'll find that it doesn't exist.

That's when the urge hits you: Have one built from the ground up. That way everything is the way you want it. You won't be wearing an off-the-rack suit, nor having one altered to fit you—you're having one made for you, right down to choosing the sheep that will donate the wool. What a rush.

You will finally come to grips with this urge after you've tried all the rationalization angles you can think of in order to keep from spending the money: It's too expensive; it takes too long; my wife will divorce me (no—you're not that lucky—but she may kill you); I don't know where to start... It won't do any good, of course, because this little brain worm has crawled inside and nothing else matters. You might as well surrender and get on with it.

Once you have decided you can't live without a custom-made shotgun, all the answers start to sort themselves out. The money thing is the biggest problem, but there are ways. The first/best way is to unload all the other guns you've accumulated. After all, if all goes well with the Gun of Guns, you won't need the others anyway—okay, but you won't need all of them. Then, an understanding banker and a little collateral—say, your house—will get you the rest. How you get the gun past your Significant Other is your problem. I did it, you can do it. I'm not telling you how; my wife knows how to read. These are minor nuisances, easily solved by the resolute gun buyer. It isn't like you didn't learn a few tricks getting to this point, and you're resourceful and dedicated to the task or you wouldn't have read this far.

Now is the time to start doing your research. You'll find custom companies that offer only one grade—the Best. These are the Purdeys and the Hollands and others. Looking seriously at one of these makers exacerbates the money problem and also uncovers the other problem—time. It takes several years to get one of these guns from the time the order is placed until delivery. If you are 55 years old when you order the gun, you will be pushing 60 before you get it.

And the cost is right smart as well—about what a nice house used to cost, and what, say, a couple of 4×4 pickups cost today—brand new and loaded, of course.

At this point, some stop looking. But you shouldn't. If you can afford the time and money for one of these guns, by all means go after it. But there are other alternatives, especially the Basques and the Italians, who both make lovely guns. The waiting period is months, not years, and the price much lower—up to a tenth the price of a new Holland in some cases. And many of these makers produce custom guns in more than one grade, meaning you have even more choices.

What you'll find in dealing with companies offering more than one grade of shotgun is that in many cases, mechanically, you give nothing away by ordering a lower-grade gun. Small companies depend upon word of mouth and also upon repeat business from the same clients, so there are many good reasons to make sure that every gun that goes out their door is the best it can be. I tell you this so that you will not feel that the $5,000 custom gun from a maker is not as sound as the $15,000 gun from the same maker. It is. Is it as pretty? Ah, that's something else.

The wood is excellent in the high grades from Spain (the Basque country, really) and Italy, the two countries making the best custom guns for the dollar right now. While Italians have some terrific custom makers, such as Perazzi, where a $65,000 shotgun is nothing out of the ordinary, they also have many small makers who will build a fine gun for $10,000. The Italians also have some interesting and innovative mechanics in their guns, too. The Basques, by contrast, long ago decided that they would simply copy what the English perfected years ago in London and let it go at that—the Holland & Holland and Purdey-style actions being the mainstays of virtually all the better makers.

If you order a less-expensive gun, you get less-expensive wood— plainer, but still beautiful. The same goes for engraving, and here cost really comes into play. The price of engraving on a custom gun, if the engraving is first rate, can be as much as 30 percent of the gun's cost. So the same gun with extra-fancy wood and custom engraving of your favorite dog or your favorite bird or your mother-in-law will quickly double the price of the gun—and the ejectors won't throw the spent hulls one inch farther, nor will the triggers let off one tad more crisp.

For my money, I'll sacrifice engraving for better wood. A little rose-and-scroll and first rate Turkish walnut is more pleasing to my eye than plain walnut and a banknote-engraved scene of Custer's Last Stand complete with dead horses.

In almost all cases, as indicated above, the finishing is better on higher-grade guns, of course—the wood-to-metal fit, the luster in the stock's finish, the crisp, precise checkering pattern with sharp diamonds and no overruns. Now, it shouldn't be that way; cheaper wood shouldn't necessarily mean less care in finishing it into a stock. But it seems to, although the differences are very, very small.

Lower-grade bespoke guns, by the way, are the ones that most often get used. The fellows who buy a real high-grade shotgun very often decide it's worth more in the gun safe than in a grouse cover where a $600 scratch in the stock is a real possibility. These fellows are cheating themselves. But it's their choice. Me, I shoot them—the guns, of course, not those other fellows.

Okay, so you've picked out a company to make your gun, you've picked out a model you want. Now it's time to start making it a custom gun. The first item is gauge. Here, there are things to consider. You may want a 28-gauge so bad you can taste it, but do you travel a lot to hunt? Maybe you live in Minnesota and you want the gun for hunting Southern bobwhites on a plantation you frequent for a week or so each winter. Can you get shotshells easily for the gauge? If not, maybe you should consider a 20.

What do you hunt, primarily? Big birds require a big gun, a 12 or maybe a 16. Pheasants and prairie birds are not easily taken by most of us with a 20-gauge. By the same token, a 12 may not be the best woodcock gun ever made, either. But the truth is, you probably know what gauge you want—and have for a long time, having learned a lot about such things on the way here.

Have you considered barrel length and chokes? What about triggers—two or one? (A hint: If ordering from Spain, go with double triggers; an Italian single trigger is just fine.) Straight grip or pistol or semi (Prince of Wales)? Checkered butt or recoil pad? (Rubber, leather, maybe skeleton and, if so, is it engraved?) Lines-per-inch on the checkering? Any thoughts on the checkering pattern? At what weight do you want the triggers to let off? How about the rib (swamped, raised level, Churchill)?

One item you must give very careful thought to is the gun's weight. You can specify, within reason and safety, the gun's weight when it's finished. Some shooters of my acquaintance have ordered guns a bit lighter than they shoot now, a hedge against the time when they will be older and, they hope, still shooting the gun. What is good weight to a shooter in his 40s is perhaps not comfortable for all-day carrying when he's on the far side of 70. Maybe you should allow for this.

Of course, the factor that makes a custom gun a custom gun, more than anything else, is a fitted stock. For this, you must know your measurements. If possible, be measured before ordering, and if you can be measured by the same folks who will be making the gun or at least acting as agent for the maker, so much the better.

It is possible to go to a foreign country and order your own gun and save money. But agents in the States do it better and faster with fewer translation errors, and they do it for a living. You can save time, or you can save money, but you are unlikely to do both, and not just in ordering a gun, either. I suggest you get a stateside agent and pay him and let him worry about things. He knows import/export laws taxes and duties, the language, and all that stuff that can conspire to turn your experience into one of those "never again" deals. Besides, if something goes wrong, you can call him.

Speaking of time, whatever is quoted to you, add 50 percent to it. That way, any surprise will probably be a good one. If the agent says eight months, figure a year. What you can't do is order a gun in April that's going to take six months to make, and then start beating every-body up so you can have it in time for the September 1 dove opener. If you want it then, order it the first of December: 6 months × 1.5 = September 1. (Try the doves chilled in a dish of Chablis overnight and barbecued until they're medium rare.) A caveat, here: If your company is one of the fine Basque makers, don't count August in your time computations. The entire country closes down for that month for a great big gang vacation.

Expect to start parting with some money at the time you place the order for your gun—something right around 50 percent is not too high. The rest is payable upon delivery. Some makers ask for a one-third deposit, another third when the gun clears proof, and final payment upon delivery. In any event, get the financial details down clearly on paper so there is no confusion or embarrassment later.

Some bespoke companies ask you to either pay for the entire gun up front or else sign an open-ended contract. What such an agreement says is that you'll pay one-third when placing the order, one-third at first (provisional) proof, and the balance upon delivery. The "balance" is where the rub comes. This can call for you to pay the difference between the gun's price when you ordered it and the price at the time of delivery.

Let's say a gun costs $12,000. You pay $4,000 upon ordering, and another $4,000 upon proofing. Now the gun is ready for delivery three years later. During that time, the maker is now charging $14,000 for the same gun you ordered at $12,000. Your responsibility is to pay the $4,000 you planned to pay (the final third) plus the $2,000 price increase. In effect, the maker can make all price increases retroactive to include all guns being worked upon at the time of the increase.

This, then, means the maker has a vested interest in taking a long time to make your gun—the better to let price increases pile up. A London maker of fine guns told me once that it takes a bit more than 1,000 hours to make a Best gun. That's half a normal work year. Why should the delivery time be four years, unless the maker is swamped with orders and he's three years behind? And from the moaning and groaning these folks do about the sad state of their craft, you'd doubt that was the case. Maybe the customers out there are just tired of making no-interest, four- and five-year loans, and then having to pay extra for the privilege.

My advice: Have nothing to do with the open-ended contract.

Now, you've ordered your gun. It is to be made with everything you want the way you want it. The big day arrives and you take delivery. Now is when the horror stories can really start. Let me give a couple of examples.

I had a friend who ordered a sidelock shotgun. He's fairly fussy, as most custom-made gun customers are. But he had a beef. He got the gun and it was beyond his expectations—beyond what he'd hoped for. It arrived during the shooting season, so he took it hunting, as you would expect. He missed. A lot.

Now my pal is no Bogardus, but, as they say, he ain't bad, neither, so he patterned the gun and found it shot a foot below point of aim. Since the stock was made properly to dimension, the fault was with the barrels. He returned the gun and, even though he'd paid the final installment, the company replaced the entire gun, not just the barrels, no charge.

Another friend ordered a gun and when it showed up, the beautiful Turkish stock was both too short and too low. When he pointed this out, the company, through its agent, offered to put on a recoil pad (he had a skeleton buttplate) and bend the stock. Nothing doing, says my friend. He wanted a new stock. The company balked, and eventually took back the gun and refunded his money rather than go to the time and expense of making the gun the way they should have in the first place. A lot of that was due to the agent, who stood behind the customer. My pal lost a year of his life waiting for his Gun of Guns, and he had to start over. The company and the agent lost a good customer, because the truth is, the best folks to sell custom guns to are those who have already bought custom guns. The first example of the bad barrels shows a reputable and smart company; that buyer will be back. By the way, when the gun with the bad stock showed up, my friend held onto the final payment. That still was not enough pressure to get a new stock made, even though you would think it would be.

The lesson here, if there is one, is to deal with a reputable company and a good stateside agent who will back you if something ends up coming out wrong. Another lesson is to make sure the gun is right in all respects before paying the final installment.

Since I've rambled on about fit, and elsewhere in this book I essentially tell you that fit is the thing that matters on a shotgun—over gauge, choke, or action—I hope you don't have the idea that a custom-fitted stock eliminates missing. You still have to be able to handle the gun, and that means practice to refine your technique. There is nothing about the correct length of pull that will prevent you from stopping your swing on a crossing rooster pheasant. Proper drop at comb and heel will not work together to obviate shooting before the gun is firmly seated in your shoulder pocket when a covey of bobwhites buzzes out of the broomsedge. And just the right cast-off won't make up for lousy footwork when a grouse breaks from cover behind you and you're halfway over a downed log.

To use a fitted stock well, you have to have pretty good technique. That's why I advise that you not have a full custom stock job done until you've fired enough shells to perfect your own technique—and birds hit the ground more times than they don't when you shoot.

That takes practice and experience.

The Dogs

Shooting Over Dogs

SINCE YOU ARE READING A shotgunning book, it's pretty safe to assume that you know something about gun dogs. Your experience may be extensive, and you could have a kennel full of pointers with bloodlines better than mine—which is, by the way, not that great a trick. Or you could be just training your first Labrador puppy and looking forward to years of enjoyment with the little furball that is, this very minute, shredding your favorite house slippers. In either case, you've come to the same conclusion: Upland shooting and waterfowl hunting are both at their best and most productive only with a well-trained dog out there doing what it was bred and trained to do.

Waterfowl hunting, of course, does not depend upon dog work for shooting to take place; the dog is the picker-up that mostly does his job only after the calling and decoys have done theirs. But upland hunters depend upon the dog to put birds in front of the gun, so this article is really about factoring them in when you're choosing the right type of gun for the birds they're after.

Dogs come in a variety of shapes, sizes, colors, and breeds. Some flush and others point their game, while others are specifically bred to be retrievers. Further compounding the equation is that all dogs should retrieve, and we have versatile dogs that point and retrieve—and also trail like hounds. All of them will flush, too, although the pointing breeds aren't supposed to.

Depending upon the birds you hunt, of course, the most popular breeds for upland hunting are the pointing breeds: pointers (not "English pointers") English setters, Brittanys, German shorthairs, German wirehairs, Gordon setters, Vizslas, and a handful of others. That's because the majority of upland birds are best hunted with pointing dogs. Their job, as you know, is to hunt cover—while you take a leisurely stroll—and then to slam into a point and indicate the presence of game when they come upon it. Theoretically, this should give you a leg up in getting ready to shoot. You have an idea that there's a bird or a covey of birds nearby, and you can get into position and be ready for the shot, which will come when you are ready to do the flushing. Very rarely does all of this go as smoothly as described or planned, but you get the picture.

Certain birds cry out for a pointing dog—bobwhites, ruffed grouse, woodcock, and many of the prairie birds such as Hungarian partridge, sharptails, and prairie chickens. The dogs' part in the drama is what draws thousands of us back to the fields and woods each fall. Devoted dog people are not kidding when they say they'd rather go hunting without a gun than without their dogs.

Many upland birds, however, can be effectively hunted with flushing dogs, such as springer spaniels and various breeds of retrievers trained to work as flushers. I would guess that more pheasants are shot each year ahead of hard-charging Labrador retrievers than any other breed. Chesapeake Bay retrievers and golden retrievers also have their fans, and some owners hunt everything with a flushing dog—waterfowl and upland birds.

If statistics hold true, for example, more Lab owners are reading this than are owners of any other breed. Labs are, right now, the most popular dog on the planet, and have been for a half-dozen years; some consider them the ultimate versatile hunting dog.

But there's no denying the effectiveness of the specialist. In the past, tradition indicated that certain species of birds were to be hunted with certain breeds of dogs—pointers for bobwhites and setters for grouse and woodcock, for example. But those days are pretty much behind us, and now we hunt what we want with what we've got. What we have to consider, as much as the dog, is how we hunt and the birds we're after in relationship to the dog. Let me give you an example.

As I write this, I have just returned from a late-season pheasant hunt in South Dakota with my buddy Dave Meisner. Dave has an Elhew pointer named Gilly. I took my black Labrador retriever, Roxie, who has hunted pheasants in Iowa, Michigan, and South Dakota.

Gilly works 50 to 100 yards ahead of us, depending upon the cover; Rox checks out every little blade of grass within 40 yards. So what guns do we use? Well, the first thought is that if you hunt behind Gilly, you'd better have a 12-gauge and lots of shot and choke. You'd also think that if you were following Roxie, you could get by with a light load in a light gun, say an ounce of 6s in a 20-gauge. And a lot of the time, you'd be right, but not with these dogs.

Gilly, in his fifth season, is a broke dog: He points, backs, retrieves, and is steady to wing and shot—that is, when a bird flushes he holds throughout the flush and shot until Dave sends him to either retrieve or start hunting again if we miss, as is our custom. When Gilly sticks a bird, it's stuck. Virtually every rooster we shot over him was over a point where the bird was crouched mere inches from his nose. As far as working ahead of us 100 yards?—no matter, because when Gilly points a bird, it almost always holds until we can get there. The birds we shot over Gilly's points in South Dakota were generally taken inside 20 yards.

Now, Rox is another matter. At two and a half years old, she's young and fast, and when she gets on a bird—like all flushing dogs, she gets after it. She'll slow up to wait for me if I make a federal case out of it, but usually I just try to keep up. In dog years, Rox is in her twenties; in human years, I can barely remember my twenties, so I lag farther and farther behind when the chase gets hot. If a bird does go up, by the time I screech to a halt and mount the gun, the average shot is an honest 40 yards and probably a bit farther.

So you can see from these particular scenarios, it's possible for the guy with the big-going pointer to actually get by with a smaller-gauge gun than the fellow with the "close-working" flushing dog. What will handle a pheasant inside 20 yards? Anything except a .410 (although I wouldn't recommend a 28-gauge for wild roosters). Dave hunts with a 20-gauge. What do you need for 40-yard birds? Right, same for me—a 12. Okay, maybe a 16 but with a stout load.

And choke? In a pump or autoloader, a tight improved cylinder or modified in the 20, maybe a modified or even a full choke in the 12 or 16. In doubles, the 20 could be IC/M, and the 12 should be a tight IC and maybe improved modified or even full in the second barrel.

Now here's something interesting: Dave's gun—the 20—weighs more than my 12. Dave likes a hefty shotgun, and the Winchester side-by-side he carries weighs 6½ pounds, maybe a bit more. The 12 that I used on this trip is a French guild gun, a side-by-side also, that weighs 6 pounds, 6 ounces. You see, Dave strolls up to his dog's solid points while I beat it after my frenzied black beast. I need a light gun that will also handle a big shot charge.

A side note here, close shots or not, if you do your pheasant shooting with a 20-gauge, you no doubt have come to the same conclusion I have: Use a stout load. I like an ounce of No. 6 in a maximum load of extra-hard shot in an improved cylinder barrel, and if it's a modified choke, I'll often shoot an ounce of 4s.

What if you hunt dense cover with a dog that will hold a bird on point? I'm talking about ruffed grouse, woodcock, and brush-country bobwhites (are there any other kind these days?). In the thick stuff, almost any shot is too close, and birds have to be taken quickly or not at all. There, a fast-handling shotgun, whatever you perceive that to be, is the only answer.

Fortunately, these birds are fragile, especially grouse and woodcock. They are not hard to kill, only hard to hit. If you hunt them with a flushing dog, as many do—including me on many occasions—the shots are longer, but still not long enough to necessitate tighter chokes or a bigger gauge. The birds are usually out of sight long before they're out of range.

Some other birds will lie for a dog, but only after a fashion. I'm speaking here of the five species of quail other than bobwhite. They run like shoplifters, so hunting them is an all-day track meet interrupted occasionally by sporadic gunfire.

Take Gambel's quail, for example. They eat, sleep, and run in large coveys, and the dog that tries to hold a point on these birds before the covey is scattered is lost. The smart money—both dog and shooter—hotfoots it after them. Any birds that flush at this point tend to offer long shots on the edge of killing range even for a big gun tightly choked. But after the covey is scattered, the little ingrates will often hold in cover and allow a pointing dog to do his work. The birds frequently come up in 28-gauge range. Since I like good dog work, I hunt desert quail with a gun that's most effective over a dog's point and try to ignore birds that flush ahead at marginal distance during the chase. But mostly I run out of breath and can't hit anything anyway.

Birds of the open spaces—sharp-tailed grouse, prairie chickens, Hungarian partridge, and sage grouse—are hunted with pointing dogs and flushing breeds interchangeably. There, as in pheasant hunting, you can tailor your shotgun to your dog's style.

The ubiquitous Labrador is as popular in the West and on the Plains as he is everywhere else. And, again, he has a tendency to work out ahead of you, as he should, but stretch that distance when he gets on birds. One moment he's 20 yards ahead of you puttering around in the grass; five seconds later, he's 40 yards ahead and a black (or yellow or chocolate) streak moving away, and you are at extreme shotgun range should the bird jump.

In such situations, as in any shotgunning, you must plan for the most demanding (the longest) shots. There are exceptions, of course, but a flushing dog is going to put his birds up at 35 to 45 yards many more times than he will at 15 to 25 yards. That means you have to plan for those shots. If the birds all flush close one day, just wait them out —they'll get farther away quickly enough. If you're over 50, they can be gone real fast.

If you use pointing dogs, remember that the average prairie bird flushes farther ahead of the dog than will a Deep South bobwhite or a Wisconsin woodcock. Even over good dogs, an average shot is still probably 30 to 35 yards.

So if you are fortunate enough to be able to hunt behind a variety of dogs, both pointing and flushing dogs, you're going to need a gun capable of being tailored to the conditions. These days, for the one-gun shooter, that means screw-in chokes and some thought to the shot size and load. A light 12-gauge that fits you with screw-in chokes and a cabinet full of shotgun shells from one-ounce powder puffs to 1¼ ounce maximum loads, and you're probably ready for anything you'll encounter in the uplands.

On the other hand, there are those of us who figure guns are like golf clubs, and just as you probably wouldn't play 18 holes with only a 5 iron, you ought to have a shotgun for everything you hunt. That's how I've ended up with things like an over-a-semitrained-setter, quail-in-the-Texas-mesquite gun. And as a close relative by marriage often points out, it's also how I've ended up mostly broke.

Pick your bird, pick your dog, and pick the gun that will harmonize with the bird's habits, habitat, and the way it will be presented to you by the dog.

Just remember that at close or long range, the best aid to conservation is a well-trained gun dog. If you don't have one, you're only cheating yourself.

Pointing Dog Etiquette

EVERY YEAR, A FEW DOGS get shot by upland hunters. Every year, scores are dusted, blinded, or crippled. Every year, hundreds more are aggravated, made gun-shy, and generally bedeviled, and annoyed. All simply because many otherwise perfectly fine humans don't know how to act around pointing dogs.

Many shooters who enjoy upland hunting, because of time, circumstance, and sometimes temperament, do not own dogs themselves, even though they enjoy hunting behind one. Shooting preserves see this sort of wingshooter regularly—the busy exec who takes a few day to hunt and has quite a bit of experience but who does not, and never has, owned a pointing dog. Sometimes this gentleman or lady—and most especially those new to wingshooting—need a little help to make sure they do the right thing.

Pointing dog etiquette is not a matter of manners—well, some of it is—as much as it is common sense and safety. It is a matter of the right, safe actions taken in the field being institutionalized into a code of ethics that have become tradition. And, as with almost all wing-shooting traditions, this code has its basis in the practicality of what's good for the shooter, good for the dog, and the most efficient way to bring birds to hand with a minimum of fussing and cussing.

A pointing dog operates for the shooter but also for himself. His desire to find birds, pounce on them, and eat them down to the last delicious bite has been tempered by selective breeding and training, which have conspired to restrain him from the pouncing and eating part, while accentuating the go out there and find 'em part. Instead of gathering himself to pounce on birds, once located, a pointer's gather prior to the pounce has been refined into a point. We also hope he's been taught to retrieve rather than dine once the bird is down, although most dogs will give a little munch now and then during the fetch. They try to tell you that the bird was slipping and they were readjusting their hold, but we know better.

So the dog is on point. Let's make it easy and say he is pointing a bird that holds fairly well for such shenanigans—a bobwhite single or a woodcock, for example. Here you come toward the dog, your gun at the ready. Now what?

Well, the first thing you should not do is approach the dog from behind. The dog doesn't like it. About the time you get close to the dog, usually a bit behind him, the bird hears you coming and flushes. Now, you are standing right over the poor beast and you cut loose at the bird. How would you like it if someone fired off a 12-gauge round directly over your head? Even if you had a pretty good idea it was coming, you would still be startled, wouldn't you? Rover likes to know when things are going to go *blam!* So let him see you—approach from the side, 90 degrees if you can. The dog can see you, and you've decreased the bird's options. If you approach from behind and both you and the dog occupy the same point on the circumference of a circle surrounding the bird, the bird has about 270 degrees to choose from to make his escape. If you come in at a right angle, the bird won't (usually) flush toward you or the dog, so now he's got 180 degrees to choose from.

In fact, if you have a hard time with left-to-right shots, approach the dog from the left at 90 degrees. The bird will now be forced to flush either straight away or right to left, which is an easier shot for a right-hander. In any event, if you come in from the side instead of behind the dog, you have eliminated another option for the bird and increased your chances—plus it's easier on Fido's hearing. Dogs hear pretty well, as you know, so you can imagine how loud the gun sounds to a dog. See what I mean about good etiquette being practical?

Obviously, don't shoot at any low birds, especially if the dog is not steady to wing—steady to wing means the dog holds his position until the first shot is fired. Steady to wing and shot means the dog holds until the bird is hit. Steady to wing, shot, and fall means the dog holds until verbally sent by his owner for the retrieve. The finest quail in the world is not worth the life of the most useless bird dog. I have met men who love their dogs so much that if someone shot and killed the dog accidentally in the field through carelessness —well, I'm not sure what they'd do, but they would be armed. Think about it.

Before you even head out for the day, ask the dog's owner or handler about his steadiness. An owner who does not train for steadiness assumes the major part of the responsibility for his dog's safety. More than once, especially on quail plantations in the South where dogs are almost uniformly mediocre meat dogs, I have pulled off on a quail that appeared to be a safe shot because of a bounding dog coming into view.

Never, ever shoot at ground game (rabbits) or at crippled, running birds on the ground. This one's a no-brainer.

What else? Well, do not, in any way, attempt to control another shooter's dog while in the field (unless, of course, you see the dog heading for a busy road, a porcupine, or a skunk, and the owner doesn't, at which point, hollering at the owner to call his dog will be more effective anyway, because the dog will listen to him before he will you). Again, this is practicality; the dog will hunt more efficiently if he only has to stay tuned into the lead singer and can ignore the do-wah girls.

If the dog is trained to retrieve, do not attempt to snatch the bird from him as he passes by on the way to his owner. He probably won't give it to you, you'll play tug-of-war with the bird, and you can undo a whole lot of intensive training. You won't, believe me, get invited back.

Never, of course, find fault with what a dog is doing or how he's doing it. Make fun of your partner's kid's grades, tell him his old lady needs a nose job, or mock the engraving on his shotgun. But don't criticize his bird dog. There are faster ways of starting a fistfight than carping about another guy's dog, but right offhand I can't think of any.

Retriever Etiquette

NOW, IT'S THE RETRIEVERS' TURN. When hunting with retrievers—Labs, goldens, Chesapeakes, and the lesser-known breeds, such as water spaniels, flat-coats, and curly-coats—you will find that these dogs operate both as upland flushing breeds and as waterfowl dogs. In the first instance, they locate the game, roust it into the air, and retrieve it after the shot. In waterfowl hunting, they function as retrievers only. Every bit of this I'm sure you already know. But you have to take different things into consideration in each instance.

Some of the stuff I said previously about pointing dogs applies, especially about not criticizing the other man's dog and about not talking to the dog in the field—although it's okay to visit with a friendly Lab in the duck blind. In fact, most Labs will insist that you visit. And that you share your lunch.

And there are a few other items to watch that are common to hunting with pointing dogs and retrievers, and the biggest, of course, is safety. Let's look at the uplands first.

If not enough pointing dogs are trained to be steady to wing, shot, and fall, then a woeful number of retrievers are lacking this skill. Most retriever owners want it that way, feeling that the faster the dog gets to a downed bird, especially a pheasant, the better the chance of recovery.

But, the minimum a dog should have learned is the skill to be steady to wing so as not to get into the line of fire. Retrievers are terrific leapers, and since they, not you, put the bird into the air, they are close, and the temptation to drag down a flushing bird must be monumental. They can get into the line of fire even easier than a pointing dog, which may be well back from the action when a bird goes up. Some retrievers do a good job of regularly hauling down late-rising birds. It is a sin easily learned and slowly forgotten, if ever. Since they are flushing dogs, retrievers trail running birds, and you have to keep up. Often the shot must be taken after a long trot or flat-out sprint, and the gun barrel can get to waving around. Throw in a dog who thinks he's John Glenn, and you've got the makings of a tragedy.

Some owners train their dogs to be steady to wing and shot, and some go all the way: wing, shot, and fall, feeling the dog marks a bird better if he sits and watches the entire drama unfold before taking the stage. In any event, make sure you know what the dog's been trained to do, and then be prepared for the training to break down at the critical moment.

Every year, a few retrievers get some shot in them by hunters trying to help out with a tough retrieve by shooting running birds, especially pheasants, on the ground. This seems to happen more with retrievers than with pointing dogs, again because they get in on the action faster, probably. Believe me, owner and dog both want and need a tough, running bird periodically to keep the dog sharp and make him use all his senses and savvy. Even with the safety factor aside, this is about the worst thing you can do to the dog. I have seen professional dog trainers at hunting clubs order important clients off the field for shooting at running birds.

As with pointing dogs, do not attempt to accept a retrieve in the field, even if the dog comes to you; the owner will almost surely want all birds brought to him. There is usually a formalized procedure for accepting a retrieve—a procedure arrived at for the sake of efficiency and productivity. If you reach out and snatch the bird out of the dog's mouth as he passes by, you'll mess up their rhythm. If the dog comes near you and even offers you the bird, ignore him and look straight ahead. He'll eventually go to his owner, whom you will both be able to locate because he's the guy turning bright red on the business end of his whistle.

As far as waterfowl hunting goes, etiquette and safety factors are just as important, although the pace in a duck blind or goose pit is usually more relaxed.

The dog will most likely not be in the way when it comes time to shoot. The exception to this can be when shooting from a goose pit in a crop field and the dog is outside the pit. He's above you, and can bound into your field of fire at the last second. The dogs I've used for such shooting are either wonderfully steady, or I've tied them up out of harm's way until birds are down and they're needed.

But the urge to help a dog making a water retrieve on a winged duck or goose is nearly irresistible. And in most cases, shooting a bird again on the water is a good conservation practice. Although a dog should properly wait to be sent for any water retrieve, some poorly trained or eager young dogs will break on the shot and therefore are out in the water and in the way when the cripple needs dispatching. Other times, a good dog is sent properly, but then the bird comes to life and must be dispatched before it escapes.

There is an easy solution for this: Let the dog's owner handle it. He knows if he wants to shoot over his dog and—if so—how close. He knows if the dog has been trained to be called off the bird so a safe shot can be fired and then sent once again for the bird, and he knows his dog's skill in catching cripples. By watching the dog and the bird, he will be best able to tell if another shot is even necessary. (Shooting tip: When dispatching a cripple on the water, hold a trifle low; the shot at the top of the pattern will strike the bird directly, and some of the shot at the bottom will ricochet up into the bird.)

The rule about helping with a retrieve is even more important here than in the uplands. The only action the dog is going to get from a day in the duck blind—aside from trying to steal your lunch—is the retrieve. I know that for my Labs and me it's a big deal, what we've trained for, and the reason I have the dogs. If a guest gets in there and muddies things up by trying to participate or getting in the way, it spoils the interaction between my dogs and me that is so important to us.

Generally, I ask a guest to stay in the blind and watch while the dog and I take care of fetching. Many times, if a bird is obviously dead, I'll let it lie and pick it up later when there is another downed bird on the water. This gives me a chance to send the dog on either double or triple blind retrieves, or on a couple of tough "memory" birds the dog saw hit the water some minutes ago. And, especially with pups, steadiness is more easily taught if they learn that they don't get every retrieve immediately, no matter how much they complain about it. Kids—you know?

In short, with both pointing dogs and retrievers, appreciate them for what they do, appreciate the owner or handler for the job he—or she—has done in training a finished performer, praise the dog, watch any situation that can be remotely dangerous, and don't interfere. You'll get invited back.

Maggie

MAGGIE'S CHIN WHISKERS ARE turning gray, and she's pretty well stove up with arthritis. Too many years of rounding up ducks in the icy waters of northern Lake Michigan have left their unalterable mark on her. Though her eyes gleam with the same profundity, there is now a shuffle and a stoop where once there was slash and fire

When Maggie was young, my sons, Chris and Jake, and I often hunted an offshore island, just a rocky shoal, really, with a few sprigs of greenery. It was the place we spent most of our days, shooting bluebills and goldeneyes as they jetted past the north point. One November day we were huddled among the boulders on the north end. There was a spanking west wind, maybe 25 knots, and whitecaps crashed on the island's windward side. Bluebills were coming through, and the lake was alive with them, like the sea smoke the old-timers called the flights of cans on Chesapeake Bay.

We had a few birds in the bag when a knot of 'bills strafed the mother line, cutting with the wind. I pulled ahead of the lead bird with my old Model 12. But not far enough, for I saw the second bird in line shudder, miss a wingbeat, and drop. He scaled down and hit the water

200 yards off in really nasty stuff, a cauldron where two bays and the wind-driven current that encircled the island churned together. The bird was a speck, rising and falling with the four-footers, and he was moving away from us farther by the second.

With too little thought for the danger, I lined Maggie and gave her a back. She had the bird in her sights and hit the water hard. The swells quickly carried her out into the chop, her head a black dot on the blacker water. She was soon out of sight.

We waited; we paced; we stood on boulders trying to catch a glimpse. We knew Maggie's swim out would be nothing compared with her battle to get back. And we knew she would make the retrieve or not return at all, because that's how she was.

Does anyone know where the love of God goes when the waves turn the minutes to hours? We didn't feel the bone-chilling cold or hear the pounding surf. There was only that stomach-tightening nausea that comes with rising panic.

After 10 interminable minutes, we spotted her, climbing each wave crest and swimming hard as she sluiced down each trough. What drives them so? What makes them place themselves in harm's way simply because we ask them to?

The last hundred yards were dicey. The waves combed through hidden boulders, rocks a young dog could be smashed against in her headlong plunge toward shore. And us.

Chris leaned on his whistle; Maggie could see the end was in sight and pulled harder, calling upon an inner strength that Labs seem to carry with them, tucked away where they can get at it when they need it.

The last wave crashed against the rocks as she dragged herself the final yards up onto the island. Chris waded out to greet her and she dropped the dead bird in his hand, its feathers glinting in the scattered sunlight.

Maggie shook herself and ambled back to the rock blind and started rooting through my day pack for a sandwich. Our eyes stinging, we turned and faced the water, not looking at one another, silently appreciating a dog's courage. There are times when only silence will do.

The South Dakota Rocket

MY LAB, ROXIE THE ROCKET, thinks that I'm on my way to South Dakota every time I head for the garage to get into my truck. It is said that dogs have no conception of time. Not exactly Roxie the Rocket Scientist, she thinks I'm going to South Dakota in the middle of winter, when flowers are blooming in spring, and every morning at 7:00 when I leave for work.

I seem to make it to South Dakota more the past few years. I have a son and daughter-in-law in graduate school there, and I have also developed fine friendships with some folks among the natives— Native Americans, in fact. Some of the best places to hunt in all of North America are on tribal reservation lands controlled by the Sioux, ancestors of the same folks who treated Custer to such a rousing time on the banks of the Greasy Grass a dozen decades ago. I get the urge to be there most often in late pheasant season, when birds are wise and tough and out-of-state crowds have gone home. That's when Rox and I head west.

Rox has all the best traits that make the members of her breed so incredibly popular. She's smart (except for the time thing) and wants to please, and she's loyal. She also has the traits that make Labs maddening: She carries my stuff off and loses it; she insists I wrestle with her when I get home from work before I can even get in the door; and for some God-only-knows reason, she always seems to be wet.

Anyhow, Rox loves South Dakota because she loves to hunt pheasants. She's a wonderful waterfowl dog, but duck and goose hunting necessitates a lot of sitting still, which she is no good at because she hates it. Pheasant hunting involves running around smelling birdie smells, which she is good at because she loves it.

Late in the season, wind and snow and the calendar have flattened the cover, and the chill factors are just a tad warmer than ridiculous. Roosters that have survived the weather and the early-season onslaught of hunters are big, longtailed birds, well feathered and colored out, spooky, smart, each a trophy. You have to work hard for every one; there are few 30-minute limits like there are opening week. The weather can be bitter, the snow too deep to walk in, and a blizzard can blow up out of a crystal clear sky, obscuring all landmarks—your truck being one of them.

There is, of course, the upside. There is less competition for a place to hunt—make that no competition, really. There are fewer birds, to be sure, but the cover has also been reduced to the point that what is left standing becomes a magnet to the pheasants. So even though the conditions are rugged and the birds cagey, the chance of moving large numbers of pheasants—even in poor years—is far from remote.

Rox and I like to block and drive, though she's not much of a blocker, preferring the driving because she doesn't have to sit still and be quiet. Late-season pheasants can be effectively driven by one hunter-dog team. If you have a number of shooters, always put the majority in blocking positions; I've found over the years that pheasants run and flush so far ahead, a couple of drivers can cover a huge area, but you need to plug every little escape path with a gun. I've watched late-season pheasants flush from the edge of fields when hunters get out of their trucks at the other end—sometimes more than a half-mile away.

Speaking of guns, leave your grouse gun at home—this is not the place or time for our dainty little, wispy 20-gauges. This is big country and big, tough birds that take a lot of killing. It is 12-gauge territory; very few spots on the Great Plains are anything but. Having said that, I've found that a 16 with a stout load (1⅛ ounces of 5s or 6s) and enough choke (tight improved cylinder and improved modified) will work just as well if I point it right. I like long barrels, as you've read elsewhere in this book, because they allow for better swings and more precise pointing. The Rocket has a tendency to work a little farther out than I'd like, so even though shots are taken in the open, they have to be taken quickly or the bird will be out of range. A light 12 or a light 16 with enough shot and choke takes care of the dilemma of long shots that have to be taken quickly.

Hunting behind a flushing dog offers relatively difficult chances compared with shots taken behind a pointing dog that has a bird nailed. The shots are longer and the dog—not the shooter—is doing the flushing. You don't know when and only vaguely where the bird will erupt from cover.

There are a number of people out there in the dog world right now breeding and selling what they call "pointing Labs." These dogs will point in the manner of the pointing breeds, albeit with less style and they don't seem to hold the point as well. Rox, if I let her or encouraged her, could become a pointing Lab in a week in South Dakota. When she's got a bird pushed between the legendary rock and the well-known hard place, she'll cock her head, lift her tail and a big forepaw, and freeze.

When this happens, I don't treat it as a point; instead, I just tell her to "get 'em," and she dives in. It seems when she does this little act, which she does infrequently, it's more likely to be a rooster than a hen, although dogs aren't supposed to be able to tell the difference.

Flushing birds is fun if you're a lanky 75-pound Lab who thinks she's the fastest thing on earth. But what Rox really loves is a good chase on a downed bird—the farther and faster, the better. Like you, I try to keep such chases down to a minimum, relying on the right gun and load and not taking ultra-long shots if I can help it. Hunting behind a flushing dog—any of the retrievers or a springer spaniel—offers shots that can vary widely. That's why I like double triggers on prairie guns: I can select the barrel and choke I want instantly. Nobody who ever hunted has been able to move a barrel selector while a bird is in the air.

I also find it's a good idea to use different loads in the barrels. I like to use No. 6 in the right barrel and No. 5 in the left barrel, regardless of gauge. No. 5 shot is an overlooked size when it comes to pheasants, but it has tremendous knockdown power. No. 6 in the right barrel tends to make an open choke more dense. With this setup and double triggers, I can shoot the right barrel with a wider pattern for close-in flushes and fire the tight barrel with bigger shot on birds that flush wild. Sometimes, even on close flushes where the bird is heading dead away from me, I'll shoot the tight barrel/big shot. A going-away pheasant is tough to kill if you're shooting at its rear end.

At extreme range, you're likely to do little more than knock him down, his head up and his feet already starting to churn. That's when a good dog earns her keep. There are few things that can spoil your day faster than losing birds. Shooting two limits to collect one has no place in the uplands—or the marshes. Someone once said that the best long-range load is a well-trained retriever. Roxie and I wouldn't argue.

As I get older, I find I hunt more and more for my dog. A well-bred hunting dog has an intensity we don't see equaled very often in our other, pedestrian life, the life of going to work each day and trying to scratch out a living. There are few things as pure as the love a dog has for being out there with us, few moments as proud as when your dog points or retrieves a bird. It makes us long for the times, now perhaps gone, when we had that sort of passion ourselves.

The Birds

Pheasant Shooting: First You Have To Find Them

When a biologist needs to handle a game bird, he immobilizes it by grabbing the appendages that the bird uses the most, the one in which he has the most confidence. To keep a duck still, you hold its wings. To control a pheasant, you grab its legs. Hmmmmm.

When most of us first picked up a shotgun, we probably learned that pheasants were the game birds favored by most Americans. We may have spent our early years shooting at ruffed grouse or woodcock or maybe even quail, but when push came to shove, it was a rooster pheasant that we wanted over our gun barrels.

Many of us drifted off to the pursuit of other birds. But pheasants still draw us. And more pheasants are out there than in the past 20 years, thanks to the influence of CRP lands, set-aside acreage, and Pheasants Forever. Many fallen-away pheasant hunters are falling back into line, just like the Old Days. But that doesn't mean we can just stroll out with a gun in our hand and have at it. Even though numbers are way up, pheasants are just as crafty as ever.

When a lot of us were younger, the standard technique of driving crop fields was what put pheasants in the air. We took turns driving and standing and waiting for roosters to come out to us. No more, however, and there are a few good reasons.

First, crops are now expensive to grow. Hybrid corn and soybeans, grown from registered seed and nurtured by expensive fertilizer, mean a lot of money to a farmer, enough so that he has no urge to let a bunch of strangers traipse through them.

Row crops, such as standing corn, tend to scatter birds and also make it almost impossible to get them into the air. The scent conditions and lack of ground cover in a cornfield are likely to drive your dog crazy, too, turning the hunt into a footrace among hunters, dogs, and scurrying birds. This situation is dangerous at best.

Hunting is a lot safer and more productive in permanent cover. Throughout pheasant range you'll find farms with woodlots, sloughs, ditches, and all sorts of standing cover that has been left alone. It is here that you'll find pheasants, if they're around, and it is here that you'll have a fighting chance.

Such hunting more closely resembles ruffed grouse hunting, or maybe even rough-country quail shooting. Tactics that work for grouse will work for pheasants: two or three people and a dog working small patches slowly, getting birds into the air when they have run out of the last of the cover. True, grouse will hold better for a dog, but the pheasant hunter must be aware that birds will run ahead of him. So it's imperative that he work woodlots and brushy patches away from other cover and toward open ground where birds will have to fly. The action will come on the edges.

Pheasant-hunting success depends largely upon conditions. A windy day is actually good for hunting—if you hunt into the wind. True, birds are more skittish, but the wind also masks your sound and better carries the birds' scent to your dog, putting the odds a bit more in your favor. On rainy days, birds hold tighter and scenting is better—unless there's a downpour.

Small patches of cover are the places for small parties—two to four hunters and a dog or two. Fencerows, ditch banks, field terraces —these permanent strips of cover lend themselves to the block-and-drive technique on a small scale.

One recent fall in Nebraska, I was hunting with my father and my son. I was handling the dog, and we were hunting thick cover along a ditch bank. The strip was about 50 yards wide. My setter was pointing and then breaking, so I knew that birds were running ahead. I stopped and motioned the other two in wide circles around the cover strip to its end, to block, and then I started through. Sure enough, two roosters jumped 100 yards in front of me, but right in front of the silent standers, and they dropped them both. I'm convinced such tactics work if you're quiet and careful.

With pheasants, you must work each patch to the end, assuming that there is a bird that will not move until you've walked through the last square yard of cover. It happens often enough that I'm convinced stopping 10 feet short of the open won't push some birds out—they have to be rooted out.

Naturally, some birds will hold in the middle of a cover patch, but they are rare, but not as rare now that the CRP ground is thick and matted with grasses. I find that the best time to hunt is early in the season in roosting cover, just at the start of legal shooting time. I've enjoyed some good dog work by hitting such places first. Later on in the day and in the season, the birds don't cooperate very well.

As a season progresses, pheasants will move into corn and stay until it's harvested; then they will head for thick stuff, and the thicker, the better. Among the most overlooked places are wet areas—places that have standing water most of the year, hold marsh grasses, and are generally difficult to move around in. When pressure gets heavy, birds will head for these areas because they're less likely to be disturbed there by predators, either four footed or two footed.

In the East, cattail sloughs offer good sport, especially on small, dry islands or hummocks that dot large sloughs. On farms, the inevitable low, brushy spots are safe refuges for pheasants pushed from more traditional cover by gun pressure. As crop harvest and weather flatten standing cover, such places become gold mines in years of good bird populations. After freeze-up in states offering late shooting, they are the only way to go—hunt them first. Pheasants will use these places for roosting and resting, venturing out briefly to feed only in the late morning and again in the afternoon.

Jim Marti, a friend of mine who owns and operates the Burnt Creek Kennels in North Dakota, told me about a hunting method he uses on ringnecks in small to moderate-sized fields. He will use two dogs, one a big-going dog, the other a biddable setter, a dog that he can even keep at heel. Jim collars the wide-ranging dog with a big bell, one that will really clang, and turns him loose in the corn. With the other dog under tight control, he sneaks into the field very quietly. Now, the wide-running dog is in there chasing pheasants and having a grand old time. But because of the bell, the birds know exactly where he is, so they circle to avoid him. What you have now is a situation in which birds are milling around, running and sneaking from hither to yon, doing their level best to stay away from something that sounds like an angel-dusted reindeer. Thus distracted, they are easy marks for the slow-moving Marti and his adroit, closer-working dog.

Early season pheasants are stupid—well, about as stupid as pheasants ever get. Mostly, they are the young-of-the-year birds that haven't encountered hunters before. These birds fly readily, comparatively speaking. They are easily confused, and if you get an old, experienced dog up against a brushy draw full of young, inexperienced roosters, you'll soon be back in the local diner having a late breakfast with your limit cooling in the truck.

Statistically, the largest kill comes in the first hour of opening day. After that, birds are wary and scattered. Wild flushing becomes the rule of the day, and refugees head for standing crop fields to count survivors.

As the season progresses, the remaining birds are isolated and confined to existing cover—cover that wind, weather, and harvest continue to reduce. Hunting birds in midseason becomes a matter of looking for cover that contains, in or nearby, food, water, and shelter. Water is a variable birds can do without if pressure is heavy. Even readily available food can be scratched in areas of intensive hunting activity; never will they be far from protective cover.

Most pheasant states have areas managed specially for pheasants and other game. Opening day can find quite a horde of hunters on these spots, and word gets out pretty quickly that such-and-such an area has been"shot out."As cover diminishes, that remains true—up to a point. Late season, usually after all the crops are in and snow is at least a possibility if not already on the ground, these areas will draw birds back to them. Most hunters will have long since crossed these spots off, but pheasants are again using them because they're often the only things around—birds have no choice. So, late in the year, the smart hunter hits the managed areas and pushes the thickest stuff there is with a good dog. Pheasants taken this way qualify as trophy birds.

Like most people, I don't hunt pheasants as much as I'd like. The fact is, I do most of my pheasant hunting late in the season, doing very little early except for opening-day festivities. And in the plains states, where seasons normally open late compared to the October openers common back East, chances are good that snow will be present for much of the pheasant season.

I dearly love to hunt in snow because birds are a bit easier to find. By looking for the pockets I've described, you can have good late-season shooting. Besides, the timid souls all head indoors once the chill factor hits 30 below. Bunchasissies.

Hunting in the snow is a treat, one that can be very productive. It's also educational as hell. Snow hunting means pushing isolated habitat. In many ways, it's like big-game hunting, where stalking potential holding areas pays off. Let me explain.

———————

A number of winters back, my son, Chris, and I were doing some late-season hunting. About four inches of soft snow was on the ground when we flushed a rooster out of range. The bird pitched into a woodlot, and we hiked on over to see who was home. About 100 feet into the woodlot, I found where the bird had landed.

Keeping the dog at heel, we started tracking the pheasant. We could see where the bird's long tail had dragged in the snow as it ambled and weaved among the trees; where it had dashed across openings, the snow heavily disturbed and the tracks well-spaced; where it had turned to watch us cross an opening and how it had made a sharp turn to try to lose us; and where it thought about sitting tight in a clump of grass, hoping we wouldn't see it.

It was really fun, but eventually the inevitable happened: We got close enough, and it flushed. Since we were both watching the track, we managed only one shot—Chris's 20-gauge cracked like a .22 in the snow-muffled woods.

Again we watched as the bird sailed back to its first piece of cover. Again we followed, repeating all the maneuvers, except that this time the dog wouldn't stay at heel. She ran ahead, pointed, and then grabbed a dead rooster. The bird had two shot in the vitals. There had been no blood, no feathers, no indication he'd been hit. The snow allowed us to find him. It makes you shudder when you wonder how many "missed" birds sail off and die like that one did.

The late season also brings a peculiar flocking of pheasants, and they flock up more or less according to sex. Roosters hang out together like bighorn rams. Problem is, they hang out in some gawd-awful places, the thickest they can find: cattails, blackberry canes, standing grass, and old railroad rights-of-way.

If you can find a concentration of roosters, it doesn't necessarily follow that you'll be in luck. The late-season bird is a crafty lad with ears like your mother-in-law, legs like a whitetail, eyes like a hawk, and given to dirty tricks.

Sometimes, for strange reasons, pheasants are reluctant to leave a good piece of cover, even when they are at a marked disadvantage. One late-season day in Nebraska, a pal, my son, and I got into an area of downed trees and young, regenerating growth in a little bowl surrounded by conifers. This little piece of cover was no more than 10 acres, but it must have held two-dozen birds—almost all roosters. The dog worked perfectly, and even with some shooting, many birds stayed put. We stayed until our limits were completed. The next day, a major ice storm made roads impassable. I think the birds sensed the oncoming storm and were reluctant to leave a sheltered place, out of the wind and all. Locating a honey-hole like that can make a trip for you.

Late-season hunting can give you such opportunities because birds are bunched in available cover—and there isn't much available. Hit it right, and you'll never forget it.

Now here's a bit of advice you may find at least strange and at most disagreeable: The proper way to hunt late-season rooster pheasants, the way to give them their due so that you don't regularly get snookered, is to hunt them as though you were hunting people. That's right—people.

The problem that hunters have after opening morning is failing to realize just how smart a rooster gets and how fast he gets that way. An average hunter does not give an average pheasant enough of what you might call average credit for being smart, and the birds—including the odd young one that somehow survived the opening-day fusillade and fell in with the old-timers that knew what they were doing—win their skirmishes with hunters.

So, suppose you had a brushy draw that held rooster pheasants, and you wanted to approach so as to get them into the air within shotgun range—the essence of pheasant hunting. Well, how would you approach if they were people instead of birds?

First, you'd probably be very silent. You'd leave the truck some distance away, and you'd walk the extra yards so as not to spook your quarry. Next, you'd use the wind to your advantage by keeping it in your face and in your dog's face. This tactic minimizes transference of sound from you to the quarry and maximizes transference of the quarry's scent to your dog. Next, you'd probably cover all avenues of escape by placing people where the beggars are likely to run out, and you'd get your people there as quietly and unobtrusively as possible. You'd also work the cover so as to drive the quarry from dense cover toward open ground where it would have to take flight. And you'd do all this without talking, following a plan designed ahead of time.

Never underestimate a pheasant's capacity to learn and adapt. This is a creature that has been adapting to humans since before the redwoods grew. Give him some credit for smarts.

Above all, remember that good pheasant cover in good range almost always holds some birds. If you didn't get them up, it's because you didn't make enough tracks through the place. Make some more.

Birds that are pushed into the air out of range can often be relocated near where they've put down. A pheasant will often fly toward cover, land short of it, and then run into the thickest stuff, where he'll sit tight. Like any light-breasted bird, he would rather run than fly. Flying is taxing on him compared with, say, a dark-breasted duck or dove. So if you push a rooster out and he flies a distance, go after him, and be ready where the cover thickens.

Terraces—steep areas between relatively level spots, such as on many farm fields—are good, but normally they lack the really thick cover birds need for late-season survival, thus making them better early-season bets. But if cover on a terrace has been there long enough to "brush up," then hunt it anytime. Terraces are best worked by two hunters and a dog, plus a blocker at the end, who waits silently while the cover is thoroughly worked by the two shooters and the dog. The point is not to have all the birds driven to the stander, but rather to have someone within range when and if the birds go up out of the drivers' range.

Certain places seem to harbor birds more naturally than others, usually undisturbed spots. Railroad rights-of-way where there is good, permanent cover are among such spots. In the old days, before effective trucking developed, railroad spur lines led to every farm town in the pheasant's range. Now, in many places, the rails and ties have been pulled up and hauled away, but the old grade, the low gullies on either side, as well as the cover, remain.

Patches of cover in farm fields are little diamonds. Near my home there's a field that is often planted to corn. Nearly in the middle of that field is a little slough about the size of a living room. After the corn is harvested each year, I visit my little slough, and I almost always pick up a rooster or two. The birds are there. They roost in the slough and feed in the corn. But before the corn is down, it's a waste of time to go after them—they'd just run into it and be gone. But after the crop is picked, they use the spot for cover, slipping out to feed on grain shattered by combines and slipping back to while away the day. That's when I get 'em.

On the plains, plum thickets can offer the necessary permanent cover pheasants need and often hold a bonus covey of quail. The key is permanent cover. Unless there is evidence that cover has been there for several years—evidence such as very high weeds, brushy tangles, young trees, and so forth—you may as well not mess with it. But if these indicators are present, you have to give the place a try. It's your duty!

There are no hard and fast rules for how to hunt pheasant cover. It's just necessary to use your head. But here's some general advice: Keep quiet, work into the wind, cut off escape routes, and approach each piece of cover as a tactical maneuver in which the intended victims are as smart as you are.

By the way, I haven't mentioned the world-famous and critically acclaimed stop-and-go technique, so I will now. Forget it. It's a waste of time because for one thing, the bird may go from a place you don't want him to leave and/or toward a place you'd just as soon he'd stay away from. I do use the stop-and-go when my dog has a bird worked pretty well but can't quite pin it, such as at the end of a brushy draw when the bird won't allow himself to be pushed into the air. Then, freezing the dog with a "whoa" and pausing myself, I can often make the nervous pheasant flush.

But as a general technique to flush birds that may or may not be there, I don't use the stop-and-go. This tactic is often suggested for the dogless hunter. I've got a different tactic for that person: Get a dog.

––––––––––––––

Pheasants take a lot of finding, a lot of killing, and a lot of catching if they're crippled. I don't care if you were the anchorman on your school's 440 team—you aren't going to outrun a wingtipped rooster, not on your best day and his worst. To the serious hunter, a dog is essential to finding and pointing birds in the first place, but the dog becomes totally indispensable when he has to go after a downed bird.

Pheasants have to be hunted with the canniness and planning you'd associate with a military campaign. You can't stroll through the woods as you can with woodcock, depending entirely upon your dog's nose. You can't sit and wait, hidden, as you can in waterfowl hunting. You surely can't stand out in the open and take pops as the birds swing by, as you can with doves.

Fact is, you can't do anything except hunt the ringneck on his turf and on his terms. His relatives have been suckering your relatives for a few thousand years. He has a lot to lose compared to you. And he isn't afraid of you—he'll live in your wife's strawberry patch if you'll let him. He's just smart.

So you must analyze every piece of cover, be it field edge, brushy draw, slough, terrace, railroad right-of-way, or thicket, before you enter. You must go in with a plan, a plan that will cut off the pheasant's escape routes and put him in the air perplexed about where you came from and how you managed to get there. You and your dog must take his cover apart: You must not leave a blade of frost-withered grass unchecked, not a tuft unkicked.

You must push that cock from where he is to where you want him to be. You must push slowly and quietly so he doesn't take flight before you're ready and in range. You must push him to where his legs won't help him and he has to rely on his wings.

Then you'll shoot pheasants.

Grouse Shooting: Let Us Count the Ways

ONE OF THE MORE FASCINATING books out in the past few years is by a fine writer and sportsman, a friend of mine named Jim Fergus. Jim spent the better part of a year traveling across the country hunting upland birds, everything from Montana sharptails to snipe in the Alabama bayou country.

A good part of his travels included hunting ruffed grouse, more specifically, hunting with the people who hunt ruffed grouse. He met with the Ruffed Grouse Society, spent time talking with the now-late Gordon Gullion, and hunting grouse in virtually every manner possible.

C. Smith '96

In his travels, he rode along to observe the "traditions of grouse hunting" with some Minnesota road hunters who shot out the window, dusting grouse on the roadside with a .410. These folks defended their traditions as handed down from father to son and derided the "fancy" sportsmen with their expensive dogs and more expensive shotguns. It occurs to me that a variety of forms of behavior have been defended with this "tradition" response, including "whites-only" lunch counters, and women-as-secretaries-but-no-higher in the workplace —you know, "That's the way we've always done it." To his credit, Fergus, the author, passes no judgments.

This got me to thinking of the ways that grouse are hunted—the picture they present to a variety of hunters across various habitats. The jury is still out on hunting pressure. Certainly, some shooters are staying away from late-season shooting because birds that have survived the fall shuffle and are in good winter cover have an excellent chance to survive—much better than a pheasant or quail that must look for food buried under snow. Grouse are adapted for snow—they burrow in and stay warm and undetected; they even grow little snowshoe-like appendages to help them walk on the top. They flat like it. In the best areas, tree buds are available all winter, so their food isn't covered with snow. Studies have shown that grouse overwinter survival rates are the highest where 10 or more inches of snow blanket the ground through-out the bitterest months. Where there is less snow, or it comes and goes, carryover is reduced.

But this works only if grouse have ended up in good cover after their fall shuffle. If they have, they need to stay there. Disturbance by predators, winter hunting, cross-country skiing, snowmobiling—any-thing, really, that will roust them from these places is potentially deadly. Lack of other suitable replacement cover means they are exposed and vulnerable.

Then there are the traditions of those who hunt with pointing dogs. Every dog owner who uses the beast for grouse is convinced his breed is the best—the coverts are full of breed snobs. I've done most of my grouse shooting behind setters, but I've had great hunts behind pointers, Brittanys, Gordons, German shorthairs, wirehairs, Labrador retrievers, and cocker spaniels.

Grouse hunters, alas, could perhaps be the biggest group of pur-ists in captivity, each convinced that his way is the best, and looking down their noses at those who don't conform—elitists, really. To some, it just isn't grouse hunting without a setter and a side-by-side. The next person, every bit as much of a sportsman as the setter man, hunts with a Britt and an over-under. Each is convinced his way is the best. They are both right, for sportsmanship is more a matter of man-ners, ethics, and attitude afield—a reverence for game—than of equipment and tail-lengths.

The late Gordon Gullion's studies at Cloquet Forest in Minnesota indicated that hunting pressure could be a factor in grouse popula-tions, especially if the area is known by grouse hunters and is close to a major metro area, as is Cloquet (Minneapolis/St. Paul). Gordy and I discussed this when he was writing his book, *Grouse of the North Shore,* and I was his editor on the project. He felt that late-season hunting was detrimental to grouse populations, but he knew that the biggest detriment to the birds would be no hunting at all. Then, public (hunters') support for the practices that help grouse flourish—namely, clearcutting aspen—would vanish and the birds would suffer. Especially since the other major factor that creates new, young-growth forest is also abhorred—fire.

Clearcutting for grouse—and a few hundred other species that benefit—is something the nonhunting public has a hard time with, but the truth is that young forests are the best for wildlife species diversity and populations.

Recently, I watched Woody Harrelson, the bartender from *Cheers*, bore the *Larry King Live* show audience to the point of suicide with why clearcutting always was bad, everywhere. His response to those who called in was enlightening to me—I always thought he was just pretending to be dumb. Some of the callers made the exact points I'm making here, and Woody said, simply, it was all propaganda from the lumber companies. *Whew*.

Then, there's the question of predation. Some decades ago, all predators were bad; today, either predators are all good or they have no impact. We heard over and over that good habitat makes populations of prey species high enough that predators are satisfied and have no impact on overall prey populations. Or, we learned that they eat other species that are injurious to grouse—owls catch rodents that could raid grouse nests or catch a skunk that is after young grouse. In a perfect world, this is probably true.

But in all the talk of proper habitat manipulation (hunting) as an additive rather than as a compensatory mortality factor (winter grouse hunting), doesn't it make sense to look at all mortality factors affecting grouse? Hunters—yes, let's look at season length. But let's also look at owls and hawks and crows and skunks and opossums and fox and coyotes. These guys are out there 365 days a year—not just during the grouse season—and some of them are fond of eating just about every day. If nothing else, a closer study might indicate that our predator policy is correct. But as Gullion also told me once, "The Cloquet area is like a magnet to predators." There are those, even in the professional wildlife community, who instead of simply parroting what they were taught in graduate school, think there may be something to the sometimes seemingly overabundant predator populations in prime grouse range.

One of the theories of the cyclic nature of grouse populations is the migration of owls from the arctic reaches when hare populations drop. The way it works, some say, is that when hare populations rise, owl populations rise in response because their food supply (the hares) has increased. Then, these increased owl numbers take their toll and the hares drop off. The owls, plentiful and hungry, head south to look for food and move in on grouse in their northern ranges where, coincidentally, the cycle is most pronounced. Then grouse numbers drop, and the hares, unmolested for a year or two, rebound; the owls go back home and grouse numbers rise.

I once had a conversation with a hunter who called to tell me I was all wet about winter grouse hunting, that it was his favorite time, and that he didn't feel he was hurting the population any. He said that he usually got snowed out of the woods, anyway. I asked him what about years when snow was late in arriving. These, he told me, were his favorite years. When I asked him further about how many grouse he shot in a year, he told me that the previous year had been about average, and he'd shot 70! I wondered about what George Bird Evans calls the "personal sense of 'enough.'" What did 70 grouse add to his experience that 60 or 30 or 20 didn't? Would a hundred have made his season even more fulfilling?

Gluttony in any form is always a bit disturbing to me, so I asked him to picture two-dozen people hunting in his area, each as productive as he was—that's 1,680 grouse from one area. He told me that "grouse can't be stockpiled, and what I don't shoot the fox will get," both conclusions out of context for what we were discussing. Sometimes, it seems the antihunters aren't the only ones woefully ignorant. I finally figured out that this man's conscience was (rightfully) bothering him, and he wanted assurance that he wasn't hurting the birds and his future sport. I couldn't tell him what he wanted to hear; I didn't know.

Woodcock Shooting

THE AMERICAN WOODCOCK HAS always been a popular bird all across its range. And there are so many reasons why: It holds for the dog like no other bird; it is often found in good numbers at the very time when ruffed grouse populations are at cyclic lows; it is, to many, delectable on the table (okay, to some it tastes a little like cat food); and it's found in the niftiest, out-of-the-way places at the most spectacular time of the year—autumn.

He can be scarce at times, plentiful at others, thanks to his migratory habits and capricious nature (a synonym for "capricious" is "flighty." Get it?). This often makes him a challenge to find, but migration will usually bring more in a day or two or on the wings of the next north wind.

Another reason why the bird is so popular, especially among grouse hunters, is because it often inhabits the same coverts as grouse, but when compared with these larger birds, can be almost shamefully easy to hit. True, at certain times woodcock can be especially peppy, such as on days when the sky is overcast. Then, being crepuscular, their vision is better because they are adapted for seeing best in low-light conditions. But bright days often make them easier targets, for the light then seems to work against them.

In many cases, the woodcock's flight is somewhat predictable. It will generally fly toward openings in the canopy of leaves and most often away from thick cover—the opposite of grouse. If you are using a pointing dog, and you should be for woodcock, you can set yourself for the angle of flight and your percentage of hits will increase greatly.

A good shot on woodcock should hit three birds for each five shells fired, year in and year out. There are days you can't buy a hit, and there are times when it's murderously easy, but 60 percent is about right for a good shot. If you can do better than that on good sporting chances, you should brag often and loud to anyone who will listen.

A good grouse gun makes a good woodcock gun, and if there is a bird that can be regularly and humanely taken with ¾ oz. of shot and a 28-gauge, it's the woodcock. A high-shooting gun is best because the bird's flush, most often, tends toward vertical. A high-stocked shotgun allows you to keep your face down and still see the bird over the barrels without shooting under. If you have time to get your face down.

The 20-gauge is probably most often the gauge of choice, and there's nothing wrong with it, but many shooters look elsewhere. Those who specialize in this hunting tend to be about the most traditional of all upland shooters, and the choice of guns reflects this, with a smattering of 16s and light 12s. In fact, it's a safe bet that most of the two-inch 12-gauges in this country, guns of 5½ pounds and carrying just shy of an ounce of shot, were bought for the woodcock coverts. Likewise, some shooters each year find that a light (6½ lbs.) 12-gauge, chambered for 2½-inch shells and shooting an ounce of shot, makes for a sweet-swinging gun.

If there is a problem with woodcock guns, it's the bird itself. They are relatively easy to hit (compared with a grouse) and easy to kill (compared with, say, a pheasant), they come up so close, and the cover is usually so thick, that we seem to gravitate toward very light, very small, very short pieces for speed and maneuverability. It's not uncommon to see a woodcock specialist uncasing a 5 lb., 2 oz. 28-gauge with 25-inch barrels. In most cases, and in the hands of most people, this is too toy-like to be effective. A shotgun, no matter what the game or conditions, still has to be swung, and a too-light, too-short piece just won't swing consistently enough that the shooter can get grooved in: The gun seems to handle differently, in some minute way, every time he mounts it.

And light guns are not necessarily faster. Coupled with short barrels, a light gun has a tendency to bounce when the mount is completed, and the shooter is then unable to shoot in the correct manner —the instant the butt is seated in his shoulder pocket. He slows down to compensate, stops his swing, starts over—it's a mess. A heavier gun comes up, stays put at the shoulder, and the shot can be triggered more quickly. Practice will help, as will longer barrels to more evenly distribute what weight there is; a 5½-pound gun with 28-inch barrels is smoother than the same weight with 25-inch barrels.

Some shooters effectively hunt woodcock with a .410. And just as there are pitchers capable of throwing 97 mph fastballs, golfers who can drive a ball 300 yards, and skeet shooters who can go 400 x 400, there are shooters who find the .410 a suitable hunting shotgun for woodcock, doves, and quail. But those people are few and far between, and they are about as common as the folks mentioned above—not very. If you think you're one of those gifted enough or careful enough to use a .410, try a little time at the pattern board at woodcock-shooting distances. You may have your eyes opened. And the pattern board doesn't even tell the whole story, because shot stringing in the .410 is the worst of any bore.

There are times, especially during flight, when woodcock are hunted after a tiring flight and a limit can be taken in minutes, with little sport involved. There is nothing to be proud of in shooting weary birds, barely able to twitter to the canopy, fly 50 yards, and set down again.

In fact, the woodcock's short flight and his obliging habit of reflushing for another chance is probably the trait that is the most often his undoing.

For these reasons, think of limiting yourself to a pair of birds, fairly taken. And pass up those easy shots, especially the kind that will render the bird unfit for the table if you connect. Ruining a game bird by being overly eager is not the sign of a good quick shot; it's the sign of an immature dolt. If the only shot you have is ultra-close, pass it up.

This little warrior deserves better.

Prairie Quail

BOBWHITE QUAIL AREN'T WHAT they used to be, and shooting them has changed, also. In the past, these birds played by our rules; today, they play by their own.

Part of their set of rules calls for dirty tricks, like sticking to the brush and coming up wild and running out from under points, something they didn't do years ago, it seems.

Some of this is due to where quail are found. America's Breadbasket—Kansas, Iowa, and Nebraska in particular— now comprises the section of country that leads the rest in quail harvest each year. The Deep South and the Mid-South no longer have a monopoly on wild-bird shooting, although it is there that you'll go to enjoy quail in the Old Grand Manner of gracious birds, genteel settings, and the refined ambience of a bygone era. This aura has been kept alive through the many outstanding plantations, privately held or open to the public, where quail hunting is a pastime, a business, an avocation, and in some places nearly a religion.

The Plains. Tough conditions: harsh winters and baking-hot summers, springs, and autumns that start on Tuesday and end on Thursday. Here, coveys are bigger, birds are wilder, and everything that moves on four feet and a good share of what flies spends time trying to make a meal out of quail. Prairie winds give a good bird dog fits. Quail have a tendency to flush wild as a covey, stay intact, and fly a long way compared to the old days when all you had to do was bump a covey, watch the scattered singles, then go to work on them.

All of these things mean you have to choose your gun accordingly. On the prairies, most shooters are also out after pheasants, and the 12-gauge is pretty standard. Good reason, too. It has the range and variety of shot sizes and loads for virtually any condition. In a good-quality gun, the weight is usually not much over 6½ pounds, and in that range it's fast. In terms of handling, most shooters find virtually no difference between guns of 5½ and 6½ pounds. Most of the perceived difference comes in the gunroom or in front of the fireplace where light guns seem so sweet. In the excitement and heat of fast wingshooting, a very light gun often loses a little of its luster.

The 12, in big country, also has a tendency to give a shooter a bit more confidence in his gun's range and authority. This confidence translates into less-hurried shooting, more precise pointing, better hitting, and cleaner kills. This is one of the often-overlooked benefits of the 12: It gives the shooter the confidence and knowledge that he has a few more yards of range to work with, so he slows down a bit and gets a little smoother. He credits the hole size in the barrel's end, when in reality he may do as well with the same technique almost regardless of gauge.

But in any event, the 12 for prairie quail also gives additional flexibility to make up for wild flushes, dogs that bump birds, and the odd rooster pheasant that, with burgeoning populations of these birds, can pop up at almost any time or any place.

Shot loads vary, but 1 ounce to 1⅛ ounces will do the trick most often. The nifty little 2½-inch, 1-ounce English loads hit hard and throw dandy patterns; so do the light 1-ouncers from some of our domestic manufacturers, especially the 2¾ dram, 1-ounce load. This patterns beautifully from most barrels. Go for No. 8 early in the season and 7½ later on when cover is down, birds are feathered out and fat, and range is often longer. Some prairie gunners load their 12s, 20s, or—for the traditionalists—16s with an ounce of 7½ and feel prepared for anything that jumps. Very late in the season, don't trust this load for pheasants unless you have a very good, very close-working dog who is also a nonslip retriever. Then, still think long and hard.

As far as chokes, screw-in chokes give you the flexibility to cope with the vagaries of cover, season duration, wind conditions (birds tend to flush wilder in higher winds, and it is almost always blowing on the prairies in autumn), and the experience of your dogs. For the fixed-choke double, a tight improved cylinder and a tight modified are probably the best. If those are too tight in close-cover shooting, they will more than make up for it day in and day out on the longer ranges you'll normally encounter.

The first-time prairie quail hunter is often amazed when he shoots his first bobwhite and steps off the distance from where he shot to where the bird was actually hit. If he's from the Eastern woodcock coverts, he's likely to be astounded that the 15-yard kill he just made steps off at closer to 30. With open skies and rolling hills, there's little with which to judge distance, and the yards add up fast.

Barrel lengths can go from 26 inches to 28, but the longer ones will swing better. The prairie is no place for short, 25-inch barrels.

Stock fit can be something of a problem. If a gun is going to serve duty as a prairie pheasant piece, it will have to be stocked high because of these big birds' tendency toward being a rising target. But bobwhite very often bore out low or at least rise quickly and then level out. The best compromise is to shoot a high-stocked gun—maybe a quarter pattern high at 30 yards—and just get used to it. Most people shoot better with a higher stock anyway; you don't have to blot out a rising bird, and with the whole rib in view and the bird above it, there is less tendency to lift your head in order to see. As you know, head lifting is a major cause of misses.

Now that you've got your gun/load/choke combination squared away, and you have confidence in it, what about where and how to point it—technique? This is a little tougher because the quail can come up out of thick CRP (Conservation Reserve Program) ground, plum thickets, shelterbelts, or the nasty stuff that grows along watercourses. The shooting can be quick, even in the open, where wide flushes mean you have to shoot fast before the birds are out of range—a covey coming off the ground at 25 yards gives you little time to react.

But a few tips are in order. Most shots will be straightaway, so try to position yourself accordingly. Quail will nearly always fly toward cover once in the air, so if you're using a pointing dog, approach a point so that birds won't have to fly toward you or cross to get to thicker cover. This will give you a high percentage of straightaway shots. Not only are these the easiest to hit, they also allow you to put more of the shot string on the bird. On a going-away shot, as the first shot strikes the bird, it slows and the rest of the string catches up. This can effectively extend your shooting range several yards over crossing shots, where only a portion of the shot string ever has a chance of striking a bird. And a quail in range is not as tough a target to penetrate as a pheasant, where you really have to break bones to bring him to hand.

As in all quail hunting, the covey flush is the moment of panic. Here, you must pick a target, stay with it, ignore all the nearby cutters, dodgers, weavers, and seemingly easier shots. You must shoot that bird, and if you miss, you must shoot him again. If you only feather him with the first barrel, you must shoot him again. The lesson here is not to shoot at a bird, miss or seemingly miss, and then switch birds and go for another. There are very few true doubles made on Plains bobwhites. They usually come up off the ground too far away and are moving away quickly. If they catch the wind under their wings, they'll bank away from your field of fire and toward your partner, thus further depriving you of opportunities.

The best bet is to think of a covey rise as a chance to cleanly take one bird with your two shots. Unlike the South, where covey-shooting-only is often the rule, and a snappy right-and-left marks an accomplished shooter, a prairie hunter, practiced in his brand of the sport, is looking to fold up but a single bird from the 20 or 30 buzzing out ahead of him.

One of the best ways to do this is to work on the "back" of the covey. Even though it seems like it at the time, bobwhites rarely come off the ground en masse. Instead, they come up in two or three waves, a delayed departure that may take several seconds, and often with a few tail-enders that can be used to advantage. So if you're pretty cagey, and you've made up your mind that you aren't going to go after a double, use the first several flushing birds as a guide rather than as potential targets. The rest of the covey will most likely follow the leaders. This will give you an indication of their direction and range. You can set yourself and then make a good shot at a target for which you're ready. The absolute last thing you want to do is wildly let off both barrels at the first flurry of wings and be standing there with an empty shotgun while about 17 more birds infuriatingly flush in threes and fours, headed straight away after their pals.

Naturally, the reverse of this axiom is also true: If you want to make doubles, pick your first bird from the first wave to flush. Then, after you have dropped that one, the trailing birds are up and moving and one from this crowd can come in for attention. Very often, when you execute this properly, you'll find the two birds lying within feet of one another, even though they were shot with a substantial time interval in between.

Remember that late in the season, quail coveys have been shot down to about the lowest point they should be, so if you move a covey of only six to eight birds, let them go; they need this number for protection and heat retention. To shoot a covey's numbers any lower than this is a sure ticket to disaster for the surviving birds. Properly treated and with suitable habitat, a covey can become multigenerational, occupying the same home range for years. The characters change, but the covey remains.

Bobwhites: They're Any Way You Want Them

THERE ARE ANY NUMBER of things I like about the South. I like the winter weather; I like the genteel, syrupy-sounding way the folks down there speak; I like the commonplace courtesies that are so totally normal—and often so totally foreign to people from the North. Cordiality is a thread woven through the tapestry of Southern life at all levels.

But most of all, I like their bobwhites.

I'm a Yankee living in northern Michigan, home of ruffed grouse and woodcock. I also spend a little time hunting ducks, and if I go farther north, I can actually get in a little sharptail shooting in the early fall. The closest quail territory is a couple-hundred miles from here, maybe, and most seasons populations are so low we can't hunt them. It snows in Michigan in the winter…and snows…and snows…

But year in and year out, I fire more shells at bobwhite quail than at everything else combined. I should explain.

The first time I ever saw a bobwhite on the wing, I was 17 years old and on a pheasant-hunting trip with my dad in Nebraska. A covey of quail got up out of a shelterbelt on my side and buzzed through the trees. They looked like tiny ruffed grouse, and because I'd always read everything I could get my hands on about quail, I immediately recognized them for what they were. In those days, I shot a Real Man's Gun —a 12-gauge autoloader—and I could make it sound like a motorcycle engine. I went to work, and when the smoke and feathers and the odd tree limb cleared, I had three birds down with three shots. It was the first, last, and only triple I ever shot on quail. I figured all the tons of stories I'd read about quail were only half true: They were great little birds, but they weren't that hard to hit.

I missed the next 27 shots at quail. In a row. All of 'em.

I could have gone 0-for-27 with a tire iron.

But I did get maximum yardage out of my triple, or The Triple, as I started to call it. I could bring it up in casual conversation so smooth, no one ever saw it coming. Like, in the checkout line at the grocery store:"I see you've got three green peppers there, mister; did I ever tell you about the three quail I got with three shots on one covey rise?"

Since I'd never seen the poor guy before, it was unlikely, so I'd tell him—and anyone else within earshot.

The first quail of my experience were the prairie quail of Nebraska, Iowa, and Kansas, birds taken as an aside to pheasant hunting. Since America's Breadbasket is also the quail basket in terms of annual harvest, I'm pretty sure that most of the birds shot there even today are taken the same way, as happy little dabs of frosting that fall off the ringneck cake.

Later, I started to go to the Plains to hunt quail on purpose and found out that this was the deal for me—hunt quail and let the pheasants be the serendipitous sidelight. If hunting somewhere that had good pheasant populations and great quail populations, this is just how I did it. Still do.

Later on, I started to head to the South for quail. As I said, winter in my part of the world is long, gray, and very cold. Any one of these is adequate to make a bird hunter whose seasons closed up about the time other parts of the country are thinking about opening them think"South."

The best—at least the classiest—way to hunt quail in the South is the old style: mule wagon; dogs braced in one-hour stints; dog handler and scout on horseback; a fella handy to help you get your gun out of the wagon box before walking in on point or a cool drink if you want one; guides with two first names and dogs with names like Bud and Billy and Junior; Spanish moss hanging from live oaks; and dinner in a place you expect to see Rhett Butler. Places like this are expensive, but the right ones will convince you it's 1890 all over again, and you really are a rich Northerner come down to your plantation to spend the winter shootin' birds.

The dog work at such places is normally very good. I was at one in south Georgia where the host had seven dogs in the field, and they all backed. It's a sight to see seven dogs all locked up on each other; it's also a bit of fun to try to figure out which one has the birds. Naturally, after you do figure it out, you'll shoot lousy.

But the quail of the South are about as civilized as the folks who care for them. Whether wild or pen-reared, Southern bobwhites seem to have their own sense of tradition and values, of facing up to it, like an antebellum Southern gentleman facing up to his opponent's shot in a duel over some point of honor. If you play by the rules and can find and pin him on his own ground, he will play by the rules, too. He'll be fast, but he'll be fair, and the rest is up to you. All very nice and neat without being sanitary and packaged. Unlike Plains bobwhites, these quail are the farthest thing possible from bobwhite taken as a byproduct of pheasant hunting. Here, a way of life is devoted to them and has been for several generations. With the possible—and I emphasize "possible"—exception of the red grouse of the Scottish heather, there may not be a more revered, studied, managed, and loved bird than the bobwhite in plantation country.

Then there are the Texas quail. Texas is the South, too. Just ask anyone who is a native—if you can find one—and he probably had a relative that served with Hood's brigade and tried to climb that God-awful hill at Gettysburg.

But you'll see a marked difference in the Texas quail, just as I'm sure there was a difference between the men of Hood's command and those who followed a courtly Southern gentleman named Pickett up that same hill.

The quail of Texas are dirty, low-down, conniving, brush-hugging, live-by-their-wits, give-you-one-decent-shot-a-day scoundrels. A Plains quail, flushed ahead of a solid point, always seems a little baffled that anyone would pay any attention to him when all these big old pheasants are around. The Southern quail seems resigned to his fate when you flush him, gallant and ready to give his best, sensing the outcome ahead of time, but willing to see it through, like the men who followed Hood and Pickett. Texas quail figure it ain't over 'til it's over, and very rarely do the moaning winds of south Texas quail country carry the strains of the Fat Lady singing.

In virtually all places, the best quail habitat in Texas is leased up tight, and those who own the leases take special care to make sure the birds have the best chance possible to escape, breed, and perpetuate the next generation of connivers. If there is any place where the intervention of private landowners in cooperation with hunters has had a greater, better impact, I'm not sure I've seen it.

A few years back, Dave Meisner and I spent the better part of a week in the south Texas quail country. It was January, and the weather coming in off the Gulf of Mexico was frigid by Texas standards and wet by anybody's standards. We followed the dogs—pointers—on the front of a truck with seats and gun racks mounted on the front bumper. The guides handled the dogs lovingly and well, and they responded by hunting like troopers.

But the quail barely cooperated. We averaged 16 coveys in the morning, and the same in the afternoon—some of the best wild-bird shooting Dave or I had ever had. The coveys averaged 12 to 15 birds each, yet we had trouble coming up with the 12-bird limit. Meisner had trouble partly because he always has a little trouble with fast birds in quick situations, and partly because the 12-gauge skeet gun he was shooting was all wrong for the habitat. I had a hard time because, even though the gun I was using was a 5½-pound, 28-gauge side-by-side double, mostly I'm a lousy shot.

But the main reason for our difficulty was the quail: We would get but one chance at the covey rise, and then the birds were gone into mesquite thickets where cactus and thorn bushes made them as safe from us as if they had disappeared into a tear in the time/space continuum and were calmly feeding somewhere in the next dimension.

In Mexico, quail do not offer themselves up as challenging targets, playing by the rules, as in the South; they do not appear capriciously as enriching little supplements to a pheasant hunt as they do on the Plains; they don't have the sneaky, slippery reputation of the brush-loving quail of Texas. In Mexico, they are straightforward about the whole thing, but with a little of everything thrown in.

The country is mostly wide open, like the Plains. The birds hold for a dog, like the South, but they don't hold all that well, so there's some of Texas in them. What they have is speed—enough to burn. The bobwhites of Mexico are the fastest I've ever encountered, and misses can pile up to the point that the dogs start looking at you over their shoulders. The bobwhite shooting in Tamaulipas, Mexico, is the best on earth—bar none.

No matter where you hunt him, you are the one who has to adapt. So does your dog. He has to adjust his range, work the wind, and stay steady to wing (for certain) and shot (most of the time). He has to worry about snakes, cactus spines, and sand burrs, or some combination of all. And you have to know your dogs, which one is great on coveys and which one is the singles specialist.

You have to know when a 28-gauge is the ticket (Texas brush country), when the authority of a 12 is needed (Plains), and when it's time to observe tradition and haul out the little 20 or 16 (plantation). You have to be quick, fast, and smooth, and you have to have an appreciation for sport at its finest.

Depending upon what you want from a game bird and your hunting experiences, the accommodating little bobwhite quail can probably give it to you, depending upon where you go to look for him. He is fast but forgiving, sneaky but accommodating.

The only problem is, you may have to go looking for him and adapt your hunting methods to fit the way he wants to do things.

But that's not all bad, either.

Field Geese

To MANY, WATERFOWLING means goose hunting. Population increases in North American wild goose flocks are a real wildlife success story. There was a time when a Canada was a real trophy; he still is, but one that's more attainable than ever before. But with increased populations, there has not been a detectable decrease in intelligence—they're still just as smart as they always were, nuisance goose populations on golf courses notwithstanding.

Geese are grazers. Over-water shooting is available, but the best and most productive is over crop fields. This is probably true throughout most of their range, and in some parts of the country, such as in Texas for snow goose shooting, it approaches a regional holiday. The best areas are often leased up tight and either converted to private clubs or as commercial open-to-the-public operations. In these places, goose pits are often rented out on a per diem basis, the field bringing 20 times what it ever did in crop revenues.

Generally speaking, geese will roost overnight on a body of water, safe from landborne predators, then fly out in the morning to the field they've chosen for breakfast. They're pretty civilized about the whole thing, though, arising later than ducks to start off. If you're close enough to hear them, there is a tremendous cacophony just before they lift off, followed by silence as they rise into the air and attain flight formation.

Field shooting for geese means a couple of variables, the first of which has to do with progress of the harvest. As the harvest progresses, geese use certain fields, subject to unannounced changes in plans. The best secret is no secret at all: Just be in the field the birds are heading for anyway, and a lot of the mystery is gone right off the bat. You must be there in the morning, well before light, in position, with decoys out as grazers into the wind.

Under normal conditions, it's best to locate your blind or pit downwind of the decoys, so that geese, on final approach, will pass over you while descending. This does a couple of things that help you. First, the birds have their attention riveted on the decoys ahead of them. If you are there, someplace among the decoys, your location is in their field of concentration, so your chances of getting spotted are increased. Second, geese passing over you at close range present exceptionally vulnerable targets—big, close in, vitals exposed.

The birds' landing path has to be examined as well. On days of high wind, geese often make long, low approaches, where this system works best; some days, when the wind isn't a factor, they will often come from great heights and descend rapidly with that wonderful whiffling motion, almost turning over in the air to scrub off speed and lose altitude. On days such as this, you have to locate near the spread, remembering that all things being equal, geese will rarely pass over your decoys to land at the front of your spread. Rather, they will land toward the rear of your stool, which is arranged so that decoys are facing into the wind. Many times, geese will alight some distance to the rear of the decoys and walk in.

When Robert Ruark wrote *Use Enough Gun,* he wasn't talking about goose shooting, but he could have been. This is no place for your dainty loads and small bores. Obviously, with steel shot the law of the land, it's a 12- or 10-gauge gun and big loads of big shot. Bismuth and tungsten shot hit harder and you may want to use these, even though their cost will feel a bit like you're shooting gold nuggets, which are also nontoxic, although not yet approved by the Fish and Wildlife Service.

As in all waterfowl shooting, you must be head-conscious for quick kills. A goose is a big target, and usually looks yards closer than it really is. Experienced shooters often pick some reference point, such as a nearby tree or fence post, to judge the altitude of approaching flocks. Many times, birds coming at you practically skim the ground, it seems. If you see them pass by and below the level of a tree that's 30 yards high, you know that they'll probably be within good range when they make it to you.

Listening for goose sounds helps as well, particularly with Canadas. When they stop talking with each other and are down to small, guttural sounds, they're coming in. If ever there was a deafening silence, it's when a flock of geese shuts down the chatter and the only sound is the whistle of wind through their primaries.

Naturally, movement should be restricted until it's time to rise and shoot. The main ticket here is concealment. Geese automatically and without question spot something that isn't quite right in a crop field. A freshly dug pit with moist dirt spread around it is a beginner's mistake. Geese know the contours and topography of the field they're landing in very well. If they've been feeding there for three mornings, and you show up the fourth morning and dig a hole, they'll know it and won't come close.

In these cases, you're better off to use what contours exist, wear camouflage clothing, and hold still. In the winter, white outfits work—don't forget a sheet to cover your black Lab! In picked corn, a technique shooters often use is to lie on their backs and cover themselves with a gunnysack to which pieces of cornstalk have been attached. Lie on your back parallel to the rows in the lowest depression you can find, cover yourself with the gunny sack, dress up your gun with camouflage tape or a camo gun sock, put some greasepaint on your face and hands or wear a turkey-hunter's face net, and hold still.

You may want to consider leaving your dog at home or in your vehicle against the time when he may have to make a long, blind retrieve on a scaling-down cripple. Most geese dropped over fields in late autumn hit ground that is frozen as hard as a parking lot. The result is usually few cripples, and those can easily be dispatched with a head shot. They aren't going to swim off, dive, or run away. The opportunity to humanely dispatch cripples is greater in field goose shooting than in nearly any other form of wingshooting. The dog, then, is fun to watch, but almost all the birds he brings in, you could have got yourself. And he won't hold still, so his contributions are minimal and his distractions are plenty. What do you do? Probably take him with you anyway. He's a pal; just remember that when you cuss him later for wiggling.

Watching birds as they work a field in the afternoon is a good indicator of what field they'll be using in the morning, although not always. Nights of full moon and clear skies will often find birds feeding well past sundown, so the morning feeding flight is either delayed, light, or sometimes nonexistent. They're not hungry. Clear mornings following stormy afternoons and evenings can put the birds on the move, and often earlier than normal. They're hungry.

Commercial by-the-day areas, with the best land leased around refuge areas, are a Godsend for the shooter with an urge to hunt geese but no place to do it. In some parts of the country, these places and private clubs are the only options, and the clubs are out of the financial reach of the average waterfowler. Sometimes the place supplies everything: guide who calls, decoys, dog, lunch. Other places supply the field and the blind, and you bring everything else.

A word of caution: The law is very clear on the rules of baiting. The law isn't structured to give an unsuspecting client a break for not knowing that baiting has occurred. The law is written to prevent baiting. If you are hunting over an area that is baited—even if you didn't do the baiting and even if you don't know it's baited—you are guilty. End of discussion. Pay the clerk.

The law says that you have an obligation to inspect your hunting area, and since many per-day places depend upon good word-of-mouth advertising about good kills, some places sweeten their spots a bit. It is legal to hunt over fields that have been planted and harvested as commercial crops and that produce normal agricultural waste. Waste from these harvested fields is what attracts geese, but it hasn't been put there for that purpose. If the place in which you are hunting plants corn and then just knocks it over near your blind—that's baiting and you are guilty.

Sometimes this gets subjective about what is "normal waste," and that's why there are lawyers and courts. But if the place looks fishy to you —too much corn scattered about—it's probably baited in the eyes of the law. Your best bet in this case is to get out and demand your money back. Tell the owner why, as well, and if he won't give you a refund, tell him you want to call a game warden for an impartial opinion of the field's legality. The owner could be right and you can resume hunting. Chances are, he'll just refund your money and show you the door.

A Respect for Game

I HAVE NOTICED OVER THE years that this country has become more and more dog crazy, and bird hunters, be they upland shooters or water-fowlers, are no different. I take second place to no one in my affection for hunting dogs in general and my own in particular; my freeloaders sleep in my bedroom—on the bed when I'm not in it—meet me at the door for some rough-and-tumble every evening after work, and generally have moved right in on my life. But we have to remember who we're dealing with, here. Animals. And our dogs are not the only animals we have to consider.

When we take a shotgun in hand and head out for a day's hunt, we are taking on an entire set of responsibilities. We have responsibilities to landowners, nonhunting civilians, our shooting partners, the law, the dogs, and the game we hunt. We are going out there with several goals in mind, not the least is to take part in an activity that is steeped in generations of honorable tradition. But since we're going with a gun, paramount among those purposes is to kill something— the birds we hunt—as quickly and humanely as possible. That's one reason why you're reading this book: to find out if I might know something about the technique or the guns that will enable you to do what you intend to do better and more efficiently and—yes—more enjoyably.

The assumption of those responsibilities—the willingness to play by the rules of law or acceptable conduct—is summed up in a broad, general concept called sporting ethics:

1. We do not trespass
2. We do not handle our firearms in an unsafe manner

3. We don't steal another hunter's shots.
4. We do not place anyone, including our dogs, in harm's way.
5. We have a respect for game that calls for it to be shot, retrieved, and dispatched if necessary with all due speed and in a humane manner.

Often, these last two can be at odds with one another. Here's a situation that occurs often to all of us. We're hunting in rugged conditions, let's say big water, a lot of wind, big waves. If we had any sense, we'd be inside someplace playing computer solitaire. But we're not, we're out here freezing our backsides off trying to round up a duck dinner. A mallard flaps into the decoys, and since we're stiff and cold, the shot isn't our best, and the bird turns, catches the wind, and drops a hundred yards off, still very much alive. The wind and currents grab the bird and by the time we get our retriever lined up, the duck is a speck 200 yards off. It will be a long, arduous retrieve in brutal conditions. The dog is going to be at risk, no question about it.

Every year, dogs drown trying just such a retrieve, and now the time of reckoning comes. Perfectly, we'll get the boat out and go after the bird ourselves—that's the smart play. But sometimes that isn't possible; there are times when the dog can do it better than we can. That's why he was bred, after all, why we bought him, fed him, trained him, and take him with us. That's his job; it's what he does, so we ask him to do it, even though we'd really rather not. We know the retrieve will be exhausting, that the dog will not give up, and that he will most likely be out of hearing and therefore on his own. But we send him and hold our breath, getting more sick to our stomachs with each passing moment. We wonder even as we are doing it if we are being responsible, if we wouldn't just be better off looking the other way, counting the bird toward our limit, and wait for a better, safer opportunity.

But when we stood to take the shot, we assumed a responsibility to the bird. Certainly, we wish the shot had killed instantly and that he was floating belly up among the decoys, as difficult to retrieve as a stick tossed on a pond. But it did not, so we have to deal with what is rather than with what might have been.

The bird—an animal—needs to be recovered. It is the ethical thing to do, and the law requires it. Your dog is a close companion animal and friend, while the downed bird is a stranger. It is difficult to place a friend in harm's way for the sake of a stranger, but that is what we are required to do, and any retriever worth his salt is champing at the bit to get it done.

Our responsibility started long before this, however. It started when we made the decision to buy a puppy. We have an obligation to train the dog the best way we know how so that he will respond when we need him to. And it is our responsibility to make sure he is cared for physically—fed the right food, exercised and worked into rock-hard toughness, and given regular checkups by the vet—so that he will be able to perform safely when the time comes.

And then, we will, as always, hope for the best.

Winning

THE LENGTHS SOME FOLKS will go to put a few birds in the bag and look good doing it. I really had my eyes opened this season, I can tell you.

Let me give you a couple of examples. I'm grouse hunting with a fellow who is a sort-of acquaintance, and we're working a ridgeline, me on top, he down below. Neither of us had yet had a shot. A grouse flushed ahead of my Lab and cut left, toward him. My shot felt right, and the bird twitched in the air, signaling a hit, but not a hard one. I watched the bird as it passed over my partner, expecting him to shoot. But the bird collapsed in the air on its own, and dropped a few yards in front of him. My dog was almost there to make the retrieve when partner runs ahead and scoops up the bird, pocketing it.

He then calls to me, "Did you get it?" A little astonished, I hesitated and called back that I had not, and that it had flown over him. He called back that he hadn't seen the bird. By then, I had a good idea of what was going on, so I kept my mouth shut, in itself an achievement.

Twenty minutes later, I hear a single shot from his direction, followed a second later by another, and then partner starts whooping about how he finally got a mixed double—a grouse and a woodcock on a simultaneous rise.

Now for those of you who hunt grouse and woodcock, you'll know that such a feat is indeed rare, especially if the chance is a true double: both birds in the air before the first shot is taken—not flush …shot…flush…shot, which are really staggered singles. I rank a true mixed double on grouse and woodcock right up there with a double on ostriches; it just doesn't happen that often.

Well, partner comes prancing up the hill with his woodcock and "his" grouse, wanting me to be his witness so he can get his Doubles Pin or whatever he was babbling about. He asked me if I'd ever gotten a mixed double and I said that I hadn't, not in 35 years of hunting grouse and woodcock, and had only really seen one. He told me now I'd seen two, to which I replied that it was getting late and I had to be back home. The drive back to town was tense, he sensing I knew, and I rather enjoying his uncertainty. There's little chance our paths will cross again for an afternoon grouse hunt; getting birds just means too much to him.

On a duck hunt this year, another friend joined Chris, my older son, and me for a morning mallard shoot. We took him to a pet spot and sat him down, the decoys all out and everything set. The first wad of mallards came in, and he stood and dropped a drake. Nice shot. The second band decoyed, and as Chris stood to shoot, our friend dropped another drake. Chris held his fire. The friend apologized for shooting before Chris did. Well, it happens, right? The third flock that showed up, same thing, this time I was the one who saw the bird I was swinging on — which was well on my side—tumble to the water before my shot.

He then turned and apologized to me for shooting before I did, and magnanimously offered to no longer shoot—after all, he had three mallard drakes and we hadn't fired a shot yet. Nothing else showed up, and after 45 minutes of fidgeting because there was nothing to shoot at, he announced that he had to leave. We didn't exactly walk him to his truck.

Now, both of these cases point out that maybe some of us can get a little too eager to achieve, that shooting is a competitive sport—and beating the other guy is what really counts. I think all of us get a little too concerned with keeping score. I have to admit to a nearly maniacal penchant for keeping track of the birds I shoot and how many shots it takes me to do so—the old shooting average. I don't know why, either, because I haven't got any better for about 20 years, now, sort of hovering right at the 47th percentile.

What I should do is spend a little more time trying to mess up the other guy, make him miss, make him think, make him ponder instead of act—screw with his head, in other words, so that I'll shoot better than he does. I mean, if you can't get better, make the competition get worse, that's what I always say.

A few years ago, I was shooting pheasants with Dave Meisner and Gene Hill in Iowa. I was having a bad day, and Meisner couldn't miss. Neither could Hill. After he'd dropped a cockbird, I called across the field and asked him if he was ever going to use the left barrel of his Woodward. He called back that the left barrel was where he kept his Rolaids. Talk about confidence.

Well, since I was obviously outclassed, and since I'm used to it, I just took a fired hull from my vest and put it in my right barrel. When a pheasant flushed near Meisner, I raised my gun, and when he fired, I lowered my gun and asked if he'd shot, too. I pulled out the empty and showed it to him. It's not uncommon to double on a bird with another shooter, right? This way, I looked like a star, and neither of these guys ever figured out I was cheating. I did this the whole afternoon, claiming every one of their birds. Try it—you'll love the looks you'll get.

Destinations

Going Places

I'M NOT SURE WHEN I DECIDED to stop buying so many guns and start using the money instead to go places where I could use the ones I had. I think it was about the time that I hit one of those birthday/speed-bumps that usher in another decade of one's life. Or maybe it was the death of a good friend who had lived his life precisely the way he wanted to—something that most of us only hope to do.

So, mildly surprised that I had made it this far, I evaluated my gun cabinet and decided that, meager as it was, I had about every contingency covered, including afternoon guns, rain guns, and travel guns. It wasn't a consciously arrived-at decision. I was just messing with them one rainy midsummer afternoon, feeling sorry for myself that I didn't yet have a round-action, two-inch 12, and the thought hit me: *Well, I guess that was a nice little three-decade romp toward financial oblivion,* and it was time to move on.

If you do the arithmetic, you will find that for the price of a nice gun, say three or four thousand dollars, you can take a number of trips to nice places or one very nice trip to a really great place. Sure, when you get back all you have is memories, but in the end, isn't that all we end up with anyway?

Every year, I try to take a trip that I haven't made before and probably won't again. I haven't been everywhere nor have I done everything, but I have done and seen enough not to feel as though I've been cheated. I have taken some fairly esoteric trips, as well, if you count going to Wyoming on purpose to hunt sage grouse or to the desert Southwest to hot-foot it after the quail that live there, the ones that run like purse-snatchers and won't sit for a dog. That particular trip is filed, by the way, under the category "Things I Won't Do Again."

A trip I will take again is to Mexico with my friend Dial Duncan, who runs a number of camps in Tamaulipas. Some shooters do this annually, but for me about every five years is right. The shooting can be furious, and the accommodations are splendid because Dial does things that way. There are doves, ducks, or quail, depending upon when I go.

I travel for pheasants every year, as I mentioned. I've hunted them in Iowa, South Dakota, Nebraska, Kansas, and Montana. Pheasant hunting in the big country offers the chance for a large number of hunters to get together yet hunt as smaller parties and not crowd each other. I like these trips because I take my dog and drive rather than fly dogless. Roxie's a great traveling companion, though she almost never chips in for gas.

Trips you should be wary of, in my opinion, are the places that "guarantee" shooting. These are normally released-bird, fish-in-a-barrel propositions. Some liberated bird quail plantations are very nice, and you couldn't tell the birds from wild coveys. These are ones where coveys are maintained and then augmented with regular, periodic releases of flight-conditioned birds. The shooting can be spectacular. The bad kind feature birds that flutter-flush, won't fly in the rain or even a mist, and the dogs have no style, trundling from point to point where the birds were set out an hour before while the shooters were eating breakfast. You can tell where the birds are going to be by looking for spent shotgun hulls on the ground.

I hunted such a plantation in Georgia once. Even the mules pulling the wagon knew where the birds were going to be, slowing up in anticipation of a point by the lowtailed dogs that went about their business with the same enthusiasm most people feel while driving to work in the morning. Before you book such a hunt, ask for references.

As a sporting magazine editor, I get invitations to places each fall, only a small number of which I have the time and money to accept, and an even smaller number that I end up actually writing about. After a couple of decades of doing this, I figure I've about seen it all—the good, the bad, and the really ugly. But every year, I get a new twist on the good and some nasty turns on the ugly.

What can make or break a hunt more than anything else, in my opinion, is the guide. Most—the huge majority—are fine gentlemen (haven't had a lady guide yet) who genuinely want their clients to have a good time. Others are prima donnas who figure I'm there to record their life histories and seem disappointed when I tell them that's not what I'm likely to do. The worst guides are the ones who want to compete with the hunters they're supposed to be guiding. I've had guides shoot my birds for me, figuring I can't hit them. I can't, but I didn't think he could tell just by looking at me; but it doesn't make any difference because birds in the bag don't make a day successful—there's a whole lot more to it than that.

I've had guides at waterfowl places show up for the morning hunt with their shotguns. This is a bad omen, in my experience. I ask them to leave the gun behind; if they need to dispatch a cripple, they can borrow mine, I tell them. If they are offended, it's probably because they planned to get paid—and tipped—for wiping my eye all day and having a good time doing it, and then bragging to their buddies about how they can outshoot that magazine guy. And they can, probably. That's what they do for a living. On the other hand, I can spell better than most of them. Having said this, I don't want a guide who acts like a manservant, catering to my every whim or fawning over me. I like to help set and pick up the decoys, drag the boat, and even clean the birds afterward. That's part of the experience. Good guides appreciate the help, and by the end of the day, on the best hunts, we've each made a new friend, one we'd be willing to hunt with again for fun, business aside.

I've seen guides encourage overbagging—outright breaking of the limit or encouraging me to shoot their limit as well. That's wrong— illegal and unethical—and I won't do it. I also don't knowingly shoot hens of any waterfowl species, and some days they are all that come close. That's okay, and a good guide understands.

As this continent becomes more urbanized, more shooting is going to be available on a pay-as-you-go basis: shooting preserves, lodges, plantations, trespass fees, and so forth. Shooters investing time they can hardly spare and money they've had to save for what they used to do for free will, rightly, demand a quality experience. But no one dealing with wild birds can guarantee a good hunt or a full game bag. A good sport understands this and makes allowances, not holding the guide or outfitter personally responsible for rain, snow, wind, or Acts of God. On the other hand, you have the right to a reasonable expectation that his dogs will be well trained, that the food will be edible, and the beds comfortable.

I've always made it a point to ask every guide I hunt with this question: If you could change anything about your clients when they come to hunt with you, what would it be? Universally, the item that tops their rather lengthy list is the ability to shoot well. Look at it from a guide's point of view: He busts his backside to put us in front of enough pheasants, say, to take our legal limit. We miss. At the end of the hunt, we gripe to the outfitter that the shooting was terrible, maybe even demanding a refund. That's not fair. One guide told me a story of taking an overweight, out-of-practice client pheasant hunting. The limit was three birds. The client shot an over-under, and he let both barrels go at every rooster within what he perceived to be range. The man shot one bird, then started complaining about the slim bag. The guide, the sort who picks up the empties, started pulling spent hulls out of his vest—all 26 of them. If Chubby had been able to hit the birds, he'd have had his limit in an hour.

Another item that is at the top of the guides' wish list is that their clients show up in better shape. Huffing and puffing up to a dog on point won't make for good shooting, and often birds won't hold while we pencil pushers waddle into range. Upland bird hunting, especially, can be an aerobic activity, given the excitement level, the walking, and —often—jogging after the dog, especially a flusher hot on a rooster pheasant. If we are going to spend money we have too little of and time we have even less of to go on a trip we've waited for all year, we owe it to everyone, not the least ourselves, to be in good enough shape to play the game.

Finally, number three on the hit parade was the guides' wish that their clients would have a greater appreciation and respect for the dogs. Hours and days and months and years go into building a good pointing dog, flusher, or retriever. Many of the dogs I've hunted behind at commercial operations, I'd gladly stuff in my suitcase and take home with me. A pointing dog that's steady to wing and shot or a retriever that will take a 200-yard "back" come only after hours of dedicated work by a person who loves dogs, loves training them, and knows what he's doing. The least we could do is mention our recognition of it when we see it happening. Then there are those clients who are downright dangerous around dogs. Very few dogs that live out their careers on commercial shooting operations retire with unperforated hides. Every year, a guide's dog is killed by a client who didn't know what he was doing.

In my business, I run into a fair number of what could be called "breed snobs," folks who figure: "A dog ain't a dog unless it's a _____ [fill in blank with your favorite breed]." I like any individual of any breed that does his job well—pointing dog, flushing dog, or retriever. I always like to make friends with the guide's dog. For me, dogs are at least half the reason I'm out there anyway. Dogs, of course, are blatantly and unashamedly open to bribery. I carry dog biscuits in my shooting coat and vest, and I can have a new best friend in five minutes—unless the guide tells me to quit spoiling his dog.

Conversely, nothing can ruin a day faster for me than an ill-mannered, untrained mutt with a skull as thick as the walls of the Cook County Jail. If I'm paying for the hunt—and even if I'm not—I don't want to spend time chasing down some outlaw to get my bird back. Or looking for him, or listening to the guide scream himself hoarse at him, or watching him bust birds 200 yards away. There is no excuse for such behavior. A commercial operation striving for realistic conditions —or one that's based entirely on wild birds—can't guarantee that nature is going to cooperate; but they should be able to guarantee a professional level of dog work.

Going South

FROM ATOP YOUR HORSE, you can feel the freshening Gulf wind, warm and mild this morning compared to the blasting Alberta Clipper you left behind just yesterday. The sun holds the warmth of October, though Christmas was just a few weeks ago.

The dog handler, born to the saddle, canters his palomino past you and your slower mount, his eyes focused on the horizon where a pair of painfully thin pointers whippet among the palmettos and Johnson grass. Behind you, the wagon drawn by the matched Belgian mules glides noiselessly along the sand trace, its rubber automobile tires smoothing out the tiny gullies left by last night's rain.

The whole scene seems dreamy and euphoric, no doubt aided by the breakfast of eggs, country ham, biscuits, and red-eye gravy you wolfed down an hour ago. You are stepping into a way of life that has existed for decades, mostly only for a privileged few who could afford it. Now, there you are, as you have been each January for the last five years, ready to test yourself again on the sporty bobwhites that claim this land and have come to claim you as well.

You're not sure what made you, a Yankee grouse and woodcock hunter, take the plunge, spend the money, and head south to the land of quail and plantations and pointers and guides with more first names than they need, but you did it. Probably an advertisement in one of the sporting magazines that caught your eye, or maybe conversations at the gun club—something. Anyway, you did, and it has become your own tradition, one you look forward to each winter, a reward to yourself for—well, just a reward.

In the distance, the lead dog snaps into a point, and his bracemate backs instantly from 50 yards away, pointing the dog that is pointing the covey. The handler whips his hat off, waving it theatrically in the air like a Confederate battle flag, hollering, "Point!" and your entourage creaks to a halt.

It's your turn to shoot, so you dismount and slide your double from the saddle scabbard and pull the gun sock off—you learned from your first trip down what a leather scabbard can do to the blueing of a fine, unprotected shotgun. The dogs are holding, so there's no rush, not like back home when the dogs have a grouse pinned and you have to hustle before the bird runs out or flushes wild. No, these boys have the covey nailed, and they're waiting for the Yankee to come do what it is he has come a thousand miles to do.

You feel the eyes of the wagon riders as you come in on the dogs, from the side so they can see you. The birds are on the far edge of a clump of some type of low brambly bush. You kick once…twice…and the covey swirls out, their wings making them sound like miniature grouse. You pick a bird that's cutting right, pass through him, and snap off the right barrel—he tumbles in a satisfying globe of feathers; you then calmly pick an eye-level straightaway and just as nonchalantly dump your second barrel two feet over the top. Dead and missed. The dogs comb the grass for the bird, with the backing dog making the find; he cheated up when you came in to flush, and he had a great view of the whole thing. Then, it's back on the horse and the dogs are sent on.

Sounds idyllic, and with good reason. The growth in popularity of traditional Southern plantation quail hunting has been nothing short of phenomenal, especially in the past ten years. There are probably a good number of reasons for it.

Because of all the history involved, this form of hunting is about as traditional as North American wingshooting gets. After the Civil War, many areas of the South, and especially the large plantations, were fragmented. The ruling class of Southern aristocracy made up most of the officer corps of the CSA, and with their deaths or disenfranchisement, much of the South was in disarray. Coupled with the overly harsh laws passed by the winners to punish the losers—as usually happens at a war's end—much of this land fell into disuse.

But a new class emerged in the United States—the Northern industrialist, with wealth and a hankering to expand into something new. Many of these were of the new aristocracy and held a deep-seated longing for the class system their ancestors had experienced in Europe. In the ante-bellum South, and just after, this class system could still be found. These Northerners, then, replaced the defeated Southern"ruling"—landowning—class, filling the leadership vacuum the War had left. Even here, America was starting to take on the class system that has endured: one's station based upon wealth and accomplishment, not birthright.

Cotton was still king, and there was money to be made from it. These Northerners bought up vast tracts and kept them intact. Sharecropping replaced slavery, but only just barely. These new lands, populated by their new Northern owners during the winter months, came to be valued as vacation spots; even the air was thought to have healing properties.

Coupled with this was the excitement of these newcomers learning more about the sporty little bobwhite, a bird that was a gentleman himself. He held for dogs, liked open fields, and came up in a pleasing rush that offered multiple targets. Quail became the favored bird for these reasons and also because the best time to start shooting coincided with the Northerners' annual winter trek south. This new Northern landed class, like the displaced Southern gentry before it, felt a kinship with the English and their country estates and shooting parties—by this time, the Edwardian shooting scene was in full swing—and weeks and months spent at the Southern plantations were keenly anticipated. Business associates were entertained, deals made, and whole families escaped the cold blasts of the New England winter.

Like the English house parties that celebrated red grouse and pheasant shoots, quail shooting spawned an entire social "season," and nonshooting family and guests were always part of the picture. This new tradition was helped along by the development of the breech loading hammer and—quickly afterward—hammerless double guns in the 1880s and 1890s. Shooting became not only more efficient but also more fun, and wingshooting skills could be finely honed over a long winter. The great American gunmakers were all operating at this time as well, and quail fields saw Parkers, Foxes, Ithacas, Smiths, as well as a number of English marques. Purdeys and Hollands have always been well represented on quail wagons. Quail shooting became the strongest thread woven into the fabric of plantation life.

Studies about this same time showed that timber could be a viable crop on these places, and that quail coexisted quite nicely with pine. The Homestead Act encouraged settling of the American prairies, the days of cattle drives were about over, railroad lines linked the distant shores, and pine forests helped feed the hungry sawmills that were turning out timber for a nation settling down to sustained growth. Timber provided the income, and quail provided the sport. As the number of sharecroppers fell—they moved North to the industrial centers of Detroit and Pittsburgh and other places—the number of ready hands available for farming became fewer, and timber became more important. In fertile soils, cotton and peanuts and cash crops became gradually more vital, but timber remained the economy's backbone for decades.

So even if a plantation was not always economically viable, it was certainly fun. Some of the best, first, and most complete habitat and game management studies ever conducted took place on some of these places, paid for by the Northerner who—even though he was an interloper in Southern society—was the salvation of the quail-shooting plantation.

I might add here that these places were also bastions for the breeding of fine dogs. Plantation folks, both the Southerners before and the Northerners later, fancied fine dogs capable of running big and sticking birds. Plantations were big places, and the bird coveys scattered. A dog that could and can cover a lot of ground in a short period of time and continue to do so for a couple hours was and is highly prized. It's no surprise that the National Championship for All-Age pointing dogs is held each year on the grounds of the Ames Plantation near Grand Junction, Tennessee—and has been for nearly a century.

As the years went by, many plantations remained in private hands—still are. But more became open to the public on a per-day fee basis. Most of these also offered lodging, Southern cooking, and hospitality. Virtually all offered the kind of shooting that Yankees had only heard of and dreamed about.

I've been going South to hunt for quail for the past dozen years. I like Southern food, the way the dogs move, and I like the heart-stopping rush of a big covey coming off the ground. Even though I live in Michigan, year after year I shoot at a lot of quail.

I'd say I'm about like the average Yankee who heads down for quail every winter. In my home state, there is no dove season, so the first shooting is for grouse and woodcock. This opens in mid-September. It's summer-hot and my dogs are still summer-fat, but we hunt because the season is too brief not to. Waterfowling starts three weeks later, as does pheasant season. By mid-November, just about everything is closed up, if not by law, then by snow. It's just that fast. The season is spectacular, exciting, but wrenchingly brief. By the time quail season even opens in the South, we're done in the North.

I also think I'm a lot like the typical shooter who, now fiftyish and having hunted for nearly 40 years, seeks more enjoyment, fulfillment, and style from his hunting than he used to. Time was, a full game bag or the chance to shoot a lot was enough. No more. As we notice the gray coming to stay, we look for more from shooting. We are completing, you and I, the evolution of a shooter from fumbling beginner through clever collector to the stage where how we hunt is more important than the bag. It's a subtle change, but it comes nonetheless.

In the South, on these plantations, the "how" of it is everything, at least on the better ones. The dogs must be good ones and handle the birds just so. On some places, pointers find the birds, but retrieves are made by a Labrador riding atop the wagon and unerringly marking the downed birds from his perch. That way, guests get to see a variety of dogs do what they do best. The horses and the wagon must be first-rate and help the shooters, not get in their way. The wagon itself—and you won't see any two the same—is a self-contained unit carrying everything you'll need for a morning, afternoon, or all-day shoot: fresh dogs, food, beverages, shells, guns, and more. If you haven't ridden a horse recently or have little experience riding a horse, it's also a great way to pass the day.

I always feel vaguely guilty when I'm at one of these places. I think about my wife back home shoveling snow. I think about the folks back at the office slaving away. I think about the work I should be doing but set aside because I wanted to go quail hunting. I think of the money I'm spending that I'm certain could be put to "better use," according to a close relative by marriage. Then the dogs go on point, and I figure, "What the hell."

There are other places that may have more quail, certainly more wild birds—in the South you're shooting liberated birds if you go to a commercial operation. Mexico, Texas, and Oklahoma, to name a few spots, all have better wild-bird populations, and the shooting can be grand, indeed. But there's something about a quiet day in the piney woods, punctuated with laughter and tall tales and the odd, occasional bit of gunfire, to set you right with whatever in your life has been bothering you. And something has been bothering you; you're a grownup, aren't you?

The method of releasing birds is worth investigating, by the way, before you book a hunt. One method, the simplest and most cost-effective, is to release birds prior to the hunt. This is not, however, the best way. The better places carry out periodic releases of birds in the vicinity of known coveys. Most of the birds in these coveys are survivors that have returned to the wild and, social creatures that they are, will invite other, stray birds into their little circle. Biologists call this "recruitment," and what happens is you get stable covey numbers. As birds are shot or predators pick them off— preserves and plantations draw predators—regular releases supplement the numbers, so the coveys and populations within the coveys stay constant.

In the South, as I mentioned before, bird dogs are valued. Down there, dogs means pointers, most likely, although some places use setters and a few others use a smattering of other breeds.

Dogs represent a big investment at a commercial operation. There are upward of a hundred at some of the largest. This means, at minimum, one full-time dog trainer/handler, a huge kennel and feeding operation, and vet bills up to your eyeballs. Plantations hate rattlesnakes and clients who have a tendency to shoot at low-flying birds.

These places aren't cheap—some charge an all-inclusive fee of nearly $2,000 a day, while most of the rest are scaled down from there. The fee covers everything, generally, except maybe your hunting license. Plantations pride themselves on their Southern hospitality, and that means first-rate lodging, food, and amenities.

Dogs are a big draw for me. I like to watch pointing dogs run big and stick coveys. I also like to watch as a blocky-cut, English-bred Labrador retriever takes in the scene of shooters walking in on a point and birds falling, then hops down from the wagon seat and unerringly retrieves each carefully marked bird to hand. At plantations, I have hunted behind pointers, English setters, shorthairs, Brittanys, wirehairs, and red (Irish) setters. I have hunted with a dog handler named The Colonel (he really was), and another named Ray Gene, and everything in between. I have been lucky enough to have followed these dogs and their handlers, variously, from horseback, mule-drawn shooting wagon, horse-drawn wagon, and every possible configuration of motorized vehicle, from pickup trucks with seats mounted on the front bumper, to a jeep with a stairway that led overhead eight feet to what looked for all the world like a flying bridge on a charter fishing boat.

And, I've followed dogs on foot, which may be the most enjoyable way of all. If there is anything better than wandering through the knee-deep grass that grows in the piney woods of the Carolina low country, south Georgia, or North Florida when the stiffs back home are snowed in, I don't know what it is.

And, in the end, that's all there is anyway, a few days in the sun to gather up a few more memories, both of which to warm you when you need it most.

Going Alone

HUNTING ALONE HAS A special charm about it, just you and the dog and the cover or field, and a whole day to do nothing but amble about and sort out your thoughts and try to get a week of the rest of the world behind you.

I like to hunt alone, although I rarely do; it's usually with a partner or two of long standing, or my two sons, who've been my partners in the field since the time they could keep up. But college and careers and marriage have taken them out of state to live except for a few days each fall, and so I find more times when there's no one to go with me except my eager Labs. They're enthusiastic, but not much good at hauling a duck boat down to the water.

I miss the guys, as any father would. I miss their youthful enthusiasm and muscle, especially when part of the day is going to be spent hoisting a boat off the truck and down to the water, and a few-dozen decoys wait to be tossed out and then later retrieved and put back in their bags. They're pretty expert duck-callers as well, and since I have a tin ear, I always let them do the calling. Now I have to call myself, but both the ducks and I can tell the difference, so mostly I sit quietly and hope the decoys do their job.

There was an island of sorts, really a rocky atoll that was a half-mile offshore in Lake Michigan. It was our favorite spot to hunt. Over the years, we shot mallards, bluebills, broadbills, goldeneyes, red-heads, wood ducks, and Canada geese from blinds in the hardy scrub brush that grew there. But in the last year or two, lake levels have risen and the island inundated, so it isn't there anymore. The island left about the same time as my young partners did.

So, I'm getting away from waterfowling a bit, at least when I'm alone. I spend more time in the uplands in grouse and woodcock coverts than I have for the past half-dozen years. I'm lucky to live and work in a pretty good area for both of these birds, and some of my favorite covers are less than 10 minutes from the house. In the early autumn, I can race home from the office, change clothes, grab my dogs and a gun, and head out. Later, when days shorten and there isn't enough daylight, I just sneak out early. I tell the people at work that I have field research to do. I'm sure if I watched, I could see them roll their eyes.

I have a light little Scott 16-gauge that I use for such outings. The stock's fitted and I shoot light 2½-inch, ⅞-ounce loads of 8s. There is almost no recoil and the patterns are beautiful. The short shot string from such a light load fired from a comparatively big bore allows the shot to get there virtually all at once, making for a load that hits harder than it should be able to. The gun has 28-inch barrels and weighs 5½ pounds. It swings like a wand, but the long barrels keep me from throwing the gun away on crossing shots. It's bored a light improved cylinder and a stout modified. If it's raining (and we all should have a rain gun), I take a sidelock 20-gauge bored IC/M. If it's later in the season and the leaves are down so that I need more reach, I'll use a second set of the 20s barrels bored a bit tighter and shoot an ounce of 7½s. It really doesn't matter what gun I carry because mostly I miss anyway. The birds are better at what they do than I am at what I do.

On out-of-state trips, finding the time to hunt alone is difficult. Very few people take such trips by themselves; they either go with friends or family, or they meet up with friends, family, or guides on the other end. But I manage to get a little time alone on nearly every trip. My long-legged Lab likes to hunt pheasants, so we pile into the truck and make the thousand-mile drive to South Dakota every year. I meet up with friends and family for the hunt, usually three to five days long. I always manage to get a half-day away with Roxie the Lab alone, working some draws or shelterbelts, just the two of us and the birds, which have no trouble eluding us.

I think, finally, if we live and hunt long enough, that's how it comes to be; a little time spent wandering alone at sunset, poking about here and there, looking for maybe a little of our past, watching a dog who's taking things a lot more seriously than we are. Those are gentle times best spent at the gentle time of day at the gentle time of life. If we are lucky, those times come to us all.

Hudson Bay: Where the Flyway Begins

THE GEESE AND DUCKS of Hudson Bay, the first week of September, have never seen a human. Well, most of them haven't. Those returning from last spring have, but the young birds, the birds-of-the year, have to learn for themselves.

It's a long way from here to the wintering grounds in Louisiana, the Carolinas, and the Gulf Coast. Most of the waterfowl hatched out or nesting here make their way down the Mississippi and Atlantic flyways. They are hardy birds, a product of uncompromising country. It's a place I had always wanted to visit, the shore of Hudson Bay, and in the late-summer days one early September, I got the chance.

The flight from Thompson, Manitoba, to the camp at the Kaskattama River that flows into Hudson Bay had been a memorable one— it isn't every trip that brings you in on a gravel airfield in a DC-3 older than you are. From Thompson, we flew over country virtually devoid of civilization to Kaska—300 miles from Thompson and 100 or so miles from Churchill. It was wilderness, some of the wildest I've ever been in, and certainly the wildest for my two sons, Chris and Jake, now grown, educated, and married, but at the time fisheries and wildlife undergraduate students. The only problem I could see was trying to get them home again.

This is country where birds breed undisturbed, where it's unlikely anyone will build a shopping mall, where nature is as it has been since the glaciers receded not that many years ago, sculpting and shaping the land. Kaska started as an outpost of the York Factory branch of the Hudson's Bay Company in 1923, closing up after five unprofitable years in 1928. A scattering of native families, trappers, and traders lived there until 1968, when the site was bought by an early outfitter working the coast of Hudson Bay. The 5,000-acre Kaskattama River delta was just what he was looking for—a waterfowler's mecca where geese and ducks both nest and stage for migration, where ptarmigan are available and plentiful. The fishing for jumbo, sea-run brook trout was an entertaining side trip.

We saw a dazzling display of bird life—waterfowl and otherwise. And we saw an ecosystem that resembled tundra of the farther north. The cold of a frozen Hudson Bay in the winter coupled with Kaska's north-facing shore keeps the terrain cold through the short growing season, imposing an ecosystem upon the land it should not have at 57 degrees north latitude.

It had been a trek to get here—a plane from the States, then a rental-car drive of 475 miles north to Thompson through the "bush." We drove because the guys wanted to see the sights. Manitoba itself is a fascinating place. In the south, grain fields and sharptails hold sway, but as you head north, there is a mix of aspen and spruce, finally giving way to the boreal forest of the far North. We stayed overnight in Thompson—you know you're in the North when your motel is on Cree Street—and the Air Manitoba chartered DC-3 picked us up the next morning.

Charlie Taylor, an articulate, sensitive man who loves the North, operates Kaska, and there are a number of things he does that I particularly like. Foremost, there is no "winking" at the law, limits, or regulations. Second, he uses no guides. Since you hunt a river delta as it meets the sea, you can't get lost if you don't cross a body of water. The no-guide operation means you are free to arrange your own decoys (already placed by each driftwood blind), watch the wind, move to intercept the geese's chosen flyway at any time, do your own calling, and generally act like you own the place. Which we did.

The first day of the season, September 1, found the three Smiths hunkered down in a blind where a mud flat met some native grasses a mile or so from the bay. In front of us, 50 or so full-bodied snow decoys and windsocks were arrayed. Chris adjusted the decoys to his liking, and we crouched in the spruce- and drift-log hide to wait. It wasn't a long wait. A flock of perhaps 15 snows passed over at 20 yards, and we each dropped a bird. Then, Jake hiked to another blind while Chris and I shot several more birds. From his shore blind, Jake mouth-called in a flock that passed low overhead (you can learn how in a matter of hours—the birds will let you know when you hit a clinker). We watched as a goose dropped, then we heard the pop of his Model 12, then two more geese dropped and a second pop meant he had a Scotch double—two birds with one shot—as part of a triple. I haven't heard the end of it yet.

In under two hours, picking our shots and varying ranges, we had our combined limit of 15 geese, all snows. It was the only morning we elected to shoot a limit, but we could have any day. We spent the afternoon hunting willow ptarmigan, exploring, and marveling at the solitude of Hudson Bay.

The snows and Canadas of this part of the world are remarkably unsophisticated in September, but after a day or two, they can become a bit blind- and call-shy, demonstrating a great capacity for learning. But north winds bring fresh birds down from up the bay, and south winds push birds north out of James Bay, so local geese are rarely hunted longer than a couple of days, greatly reducing the wise-up factor.

The region's solitude allows a waterfowler to really hunt without human interference. There is no wondering what the local crop harvest progress is—there is none. There is no fidgeting while waiting to find out your place in the draw for a blind, no fretting that someone else will beat you to a choice spot in the pre-dawn because there isn't anyone else. There are only geese and sky, wind and weather, the things a wildfowler used to worry about years before in a slower, less obstructed era.

There is something else, too, about this corner of the world, something about being a hundred air miles from the next closest human being, about having your own safety determined not by traffic accidents or drive-by shooting statistics or grams of fat in your diet. It is good to know that there are still places where your comfort and safety are in your own hands and the hands of nature and not others. The shore of Hudson Bay is elemental and basic. Storms sweep in and make you cold and sometimes wet, and always aware that you are small.

But the shooting. Some days, mornings are more productive, some days the evenings. Some days birds trade along the ocean shore, other days they hug the inland treeline. A wildfowler has to be ready to move to get where the birds want to be. Experienced hunters can learn much from these geese, because without human intervention to affect their behavior, the geese act naturally.

When you travel to a place this remote, you have to be prepared by bringing everything with you, and we did. I could have used some more warm clothes—it snowed a bit on two of the days—but griping about how cold I am to my sons is part of our family tradition. I am afflicted with low blood pressure and a slow pulse, a sure way to get cold in a goose blind, and a source of never-ending delight to Chris and Jake. I had elected not to pack heavy gloves, telling the guys that it couldn't be that cold in early September, and weight restrictions apply on the DC-3. Pack an extra bottle of whiskey and forget the gloves—That's what I say. The first day out, I was moaning about my cold hands when Chris produced my heavy mitts and offered to rent them to me, payable in U.S. funds.

Most traveling wingshooters, those with the curiosity and zeal to see what's on the other side of the river, don't often return to a place once they've been there, preferring to sample something new. I'm no different. But in the case of Kaska, I'd go back—time and again.

South Texas Quail

THERE ARE A COUPLE WAYS, and only a couple, to hunt bobwhite quail. One way is to strike off across the country on foot or horseback, following the dogs.

Another way is to follow the dogs in some sort of conveyance—a truck, jeep, or the traditional mule- or horse-drawn wagon. This allows you to cover a lot of ground in a day, use a lot of dogs, and see a lot of quail. These are three pretty good reasons.

But in places where the traditional mule wagon is still used, wild quail are few and far between; mostly, they are liberated birds, and the experience is, for some, artificial—although I've been in plenty of places where liberated birds have slickered me as often as wild birds do. So if you want to cover a lot of ground in a day, use a lot of dogs, and see a lot of quail, and you want those birds to be wild, that means you use the truck or jeep, and you go to south Texas.

In order for this to work, and what has made this method of hunting quail a localized tradition, depends upon five factors:

1. Huge expanses of land unbroken by fences are needed, which is why you don't follow dogs across the 160-acre farms of the Midwest in a truck;
2. A bird that will hold for a pointing dog, at least most of the time —which is why you don't hunt pheasants this way;
3. Land has to be suitable terrain, no rocky coulees and such— which is why you don't (at least very often) hunt Hungarian partridge in Montana from a truck;

4. Being a long way from the closest convenience store or other civilization, far enough to make these self-contained rigs necessary, such as it is in south Texas;

5. A resident population of wackos who are willing to spend ungodly gobs of money on this way of life for the land, the dogs, and the conveyance. That, of course, means Texans.

And no two are alike—the rigs, I mean, although that's also true of Texans. One fellow from Kingsville with whom I hunted, John Howe, had a truck made from a converted Volkswagen bus that features, among other things, both a buzzer and a light to tell him if he left a dog watering dish on the ground; a fold-down cleaning table, complete with light; ditto a fold-down bar for a little after-hunt refreshment; a winch; a jack; running water; built-in coffee thermos; roll-bar; cages for seven dogs; and a seat to ride on you'd expect to find in a pretty nice car.

Gary Lockee runs the Bird Dog Hall of Fame in Grand Junction, Tennessee, and with his lovely wife, Sally, spends several weeks a year in south Texas hunting and training dogs on his quail lease. Gary's rig features a couple of chairs mounted atop his truck that command a view for a half-mile, much like the flying bridge on a charter boat. Five tons of truck and steel girders in pursuit of a six-ounce bird that must wonder what the hell is going on.

I can hear the grouse and woodcock and pheasant hunters now, snorting, "So, you ride after the dogs in a truck. Not me. I like to walk for my birds." Well, as I mentioned above, the concept is no different than the traditional quail wagon of the South—a self-contained hunting caravan that can sustain a party of gunners and a parcel of dogs for a full day's sport far from any conveniences or, indeed, necessities. You have to bring those with you. And since these dogs are used to running hard for anywhere from 20 minutes to an hour, you have to have fresh braces ready. How are you going to do that hunting on foot?

But there's plenty of walking, too; don't let that bother you. In south Texas, when the dogs go on point and you dismount and load up, singles can go anywhere, and chances of finding another covey while you're on the ground are excellent.

This can lead to a little extracurricular activity called "losing the truck." The hunting leases are pastures—yes, real grassy, mesquite-studded cattle pastures—20,000 to 25,000 acres in size, and there are zero reference points. If you lose the truck, you get to walk even more.

The same fellow, John Howe of the converted Volkswagen, developed and markets a siren device that blows every eight minutes or whatever you want so you can tell where you left your ride home. The country is flat, and the mesquite motts (clumps) obscure your view. More than once, while we were on foot chasing the dogs that were chasing the singles, we lost track of the vehicle. My shooting buddy, Dave Meisner, and I looked at each other, and he said, "On three, point toward the truck. One, two, three." We were pointing in opposite directions. We asked John, "Hey, John, where's the truck?" He pointed in a third direction. Just about then, the siren went off from the fourth point on the compass.

Hunting quail in the south of Texas is, by any measure, an expensive proposition. Virtually no land is open to public hunting, so ground is leased from big landholders such as the King Ranch and the Kenedy Ranch. This leasing makes these corporate outfits more money per acre than the cattle they run on the same pastures. The cattle, in fact, graze the grass to the right height for quail habitat, so the two coexist nicely. You'll rarely see any of them, though. They're as ghostly and spooky as kudu.

There are separate lease charges on the same land for quail and deer. Deer leases also carry the rights to hunt feral hogs and javelina or peccary, the nasty little native pigs that can—and sometimes do—carve up a bird dog.

Because of this expense, leases are shared by a number of like-minded folks, and harvest is strictly regulated by these leaseholding "clubs." All regulations have to be followed—the lease is shot only on certain days of the week, and guest visits are regulated. Every bird taken is recorded in books for the state and for the landowner.

But the lease is available year around for dog training, for dove shooting early in the season, and for generally hanging out with other dog people. On the better leases, there are waiting lists of prospective members several years long.

If you are going to have a lease investment, and you keep, train, and feed maybe eight to a dozen bird dogs, you're going to want to work your land and your dogs to the extent that your time permits, and that's where these rigs come in, each as individual as its creator.

What's the shooting like on these leases? Well, the quail just don't play fair. They head for the thick stuff after the initial covey rise—cover where everything picks, sticks, stabs, or bites. The birds are small, though not as small as the bobwhites of Mexico, and the flushes thunderous, even in the big country of south Texas. But good dogs are good because they can hold their birds; I rarely need anything stouter than a 20-gauge with ⅞ ounce of No. 8 shot. Very civilized.

Sometimes, the shooting can be nothing short of fantastic; one day on the Lockee's 24,000-acre lease was all it took to prove it. Hunting leisurely, taking a lot of photographs, and admiring and watching Gary's string of dogs—and Sally's black Lab who was called off the truck for the tough retrieving jobs—we moved 20 coveys. That we were a few birds short of the 15-bird limit per gun was due to the Texas wind and the fact that there's a lot of it around each quail.

Back home in Michigan, the temperature was hovering around zero and my wife couldn't get the snowplow guy to come dig out the driveway, while I was hunting in a vest and shirtsleeves. All of this makes south Texas a place to look at very carefully when shooting seasons close down in the North, and you've still got the urge to watch a few dogs do what they do best.

The Prairies

I'VE ALWAYS FELT I COULD live about anywhere and not think I was being cheated. I like the North, where I live now, but I've lived and enjoyed myself in the East, the West, and I've spent a lot of time in the South. But if I had to pick out a spot to move to right now, it would probably be the Plains—the Great American Desert.

Each area of the country has its own birds and its own brand of sport, but there's something about the prairie that makes it special. The big, wide sky, the wind—I love the wind—and the native birds, the sharptails and the prairie chickens. Hunting them is a trip into the past. These birds are American treasures.

Having said that, I'll now recant at least a bit of it and tell you that if I were forced to spend the rest of my life hunting only the imported Hungarian partridge on the Montana prairies, I'd probably not complain a bit. Huns are covey birds, but they're civilized about it, normally staying together as a group after they're flushed so you can get them up again if you miss, which I generally do. They are fast, tricky targets, unbeatable on the table, and test a pointing dog more than any covey of bobwhites that ever lived.

My friends, Ben Williams and Chuck Johnson, live in Montana, and I hunt with them, Ben's Brittanys, and Chuck's wirehairs. Ben has been hunting Huns with Brittanys for more than 35 years and has forgotten more about the birds than most biologists know. He watches their nests in the spring, works his dogs on the young birds in the summer, and hunts them in the fall.

Ben told me that he figures he knows the whereabouts of 500 coveys at any one time. Hun coveys, like bobwhite coveys, are often multigenerational, the same covey in place year after year, even though the individuals change. Ben knows where the birds will be at any given time of the day, which way the covey will fly when flushed, and where they're likely to set down. A top outdoor photographer, he doesn't shoot that much anymore, preferring to guide friends and take pictures. He also holds his guests to the "Williams Limit"—four Huns and two sharptails instead of the state-allowed eight and four, which is fine with me.

Ben has a unique way of hunting these birds and big country with dogs—he empties his kennel. It is not unusual for him to turn out five, six, seven, even eight dogs at a time. His Brittanys point and back naturally, and they run big. When one dog sticks a covey, the rest will back. With that many dogs, it's sometimes tough to figure out who's got the birds, but that's part of the fun.

Huns come off the ground at a fairly good range, the average being, I'd say, 20 yards if the point is solid. That means the first shot will be in the neighborhood of 30 yards, and a follow-up chance will come at 40. Since Huns are small, the combination of a small bird and extreme range means, generally, a pretty good shot load and tight chokes. Not because Huns take a lot of killing, but because you need to make sure you have adequate pattern density or the birds will fly right through it or, worse, be feathered and maybe lost. Probably more birds are taken with 12-gauge guns and 1¼ ounces of shot than anything else. Ben shoots a 20, but he shoots 3-inch magnums. Because of the range, you'll probably never destroy a bird, even with this much shot. I like 1⅛ ounces of 7½s, and I get that from either a light 12 or a 16-gauge.

Another reason I love the prairies is the people. It seems they haven't been PCed to the point that every male occupant meticulously works to stay in touch with his feminine side. Hunting and shooting are still regarded as virtuous pastimes, and those who do it are not to be feared and loathed. Check your anthropology: Men hunt—and so, increasingly, do a lot of women. In Montana, they accept that better than in some parts of the country where fellows with wrist bracelets, $200 haircuts, and carefully cultivated two-day stubble (to perhaps prove to themselves that they are, after all, male) shed real, salty tears for the fuzzy-faced deer and pretty birds. These are the same people who see nothing wrong with the President playing, as a fellow I know commented, slap-and-tickle in the Oval Office on government time and, I assume, furniture. Their hearts bleed for convicted axe murderers who should have their sentences commuted because they may have done it, but they didn't really enjoy it. They would also, make no mistake about it—these "lifestyle Nazis," as they have been called—like to see you and me dead because we hunt, their protestations against violence aside. You don't see any of that in Montana; at least, I haven't.

Still, the lure that makes me want to go back and see Ben and Chuck every fall is the country. They hunt big country. *Huge* country. More than once, I've stopped on a hilltop and, turning 360 degrees, have not seen a sign of other humans—not a fence, a power line, a jet contrail, a cell phone tower, a road, nothing. At any one time, you can see an area the size of Bosnia, and no evidence that anyone else has even stepped on the planet.

As we approach the millenium and all the problems that may bring with it, and the earth's population moves inexorably toward six billion, it's inconceivable to most people from the crowded East or the Left Coast that such land still exists. But it does. On the prairies.

Picking Your Trip

IF, AS SOMEONE SAID, an experience is part anticipation, part realization, and part memory, the anticipation—and the planning—certainly take up the most time. What you get from your trip is usually in direct proportion to the planning you put into it, and the type of trip it is.

There are three basic types of shooting trips. Trip number one is the easiest and involves having a friend or family with connections at the destination. You pack up and head for a home-away-from-home for a few days. Such trips are normally inexpensive and pretty secure. Anyone who has tried to get permission in Iowa or Nebraska to hunt a stranger's land on Thanksgiving weekend has heard, "I'd like to let you, but my son [nephew/son-in-law/uncle/grandson/etc.] and a few of his friends are coming in to hunt the place over the holiday." That's a situation where the absentee hunter has things sewed up.

The second type of trip involves picking a location, calling and writing ahead, trying to arrange for available land to hunt on, checking out the local publicly accessible lands, reserving a place to stay that will accept our half-trained mutts, and then going.

This trip holds the lure of being fairly inexpensive, but it carries the risk of being a bust—overcrowded hunting, no lands available to hunt when you get there, finding the birds, and so forth. This type of trip can be greatly assisted by the hiring of a guide for a few days, a cheap investment. Many states with a large amount of public land see out-of-staters come in under this type of arrangement—a straight freelance basis. Very often, parties of hunters return to the same place year after year, and in effect become family members, so the hunt becomes more like the first kind described.

The last type, trip number 3, involves the hiring of a competent outfitter who arranges everything, including, in some cases, transportation from your home and back if you wish. In many cases, the outfitter tells you, "Be at Point A on the fifteenth of the month at 1:00, and I'll take you from there." In any event, he handles the duties in exchange for money. He arranges for licenses, gun permits if needed, handles the language barrier on out-of-country trips, employs guides, often provides dogs, has shotshells, places to hunt, transportation, food, lodging, after-the-hunt refreshment, and all the necessary gear you'll need. He also gets a healthy sum for this service.

Some of the places an outfitter arranges to take you belong to others, and he's leasing rights, such as an English country estate driven shoot or a sunflower field in Mexico where dove shooting takes place. In other cases, the outfitter's property is the destination, such as

Southern quail plantations or the pheasant farms that are growing more popular in the plains states.

Now in each case, from close-to-home to the outfitter-arranged trip, cost is a factor, as well it should be. After all, we only have so much of it we are willing (allowed) to spend on guns, dogs, licenses, and related frivolities.

But lots of things are money—time is money; a busted trip, no matter how cheap, is a waste; expended vacation time is money; time away from your business or practice is money. One of the reasons I advocate the use of fine guns is because, in many ways in the long run, the are a bargain. They break less, last forever unless you lose them, and hold their resale—or at least their original—value. Sometimes, it's better to spend money and get what you want than try to save and get nothing at all or be disappointed.

Let's apply this to trips. If you live in a great spot, hunt as much as you want, and have little desire for something more exotic, more power to you. If you have relatives that own a portion of the state of Kansas or Montana who love to have you drop in for a couple weeks in the fall, ditto. If you are like the rest of us, you can either take a chance on planning your own trip, or you can hire it done.

Since this is a sort of tally sheet, let's see some costs and look at the bottom line.

Trip A: You Plan

Trip: Iowa pheasant hunt. Three days hunting time, two days travel time.

Destination: Central Iowa

Departure Point: 1,000 miles away, any direction

Costs: Gas (round trip and while hunting) $160
Food/Drink $200
Lodging $175
Licenses ....$ 65
Total $600

If you share this with another hunter, the costs of gas and lodging will be halved. This is bare minimum for food, gas, and lodging, and does not count daily fees many farmers are starting to charge for hunting. Daily fees can range from $20 to $75 per hunter per day.

Now, you have arrived. Perhaps it takes you most of a day to get oriented to the area and find a place to hunt. This leaves you a 2½-day hunt. The Iowa limit is three pheasants a day, so the limit is nine for your trip. If you are hunting alone, pheasants would cost you, minimally, $67 each. With daily fees and more extravagant living and dining, perhaps hiring a guide for one day, the birds could easily cost $80 each. If you hunt with a friend and share costs, birds will range in price from $48 to $60.

If we priced these things out, none of us would be allowed to hunt, but since the knock on outfitters is often cost, we must look at it from that angle.

But what happens if you get shut out—can't find land, the land holds no birds, the birds are spooky, or any of the dozens of things that can go wrong on a trip? Well, the price of a pheasant dinner just went up, didn't it?

Trip B: With an Outfitter

Costs: Gas (no driving in-state because . . . .$ 125
   the outfitter handles that)
  Food, lodging, guide service,
   use of dogs if needed, bird-cleaning,
   hunting fees ($350/day) $1050
  Licenses . . . .$ 65
  Total $1240

For this amount, you will more than likely shoot your nine Iowa pheasants, pricing them at $137.77 each. They are expensive, but the shooting is pretty much assured. You have little wasted time or effort, and you will have a place to hunt that is most likely yours alone. You'll probably eat and sleep better, too, than if you did it on your own.

Like almost everything else in life, we can save time or we can save money, but we most likely won't save both. In the case of the outfitter's hunt, you pay money in order to be immediately productive—having fun—hunting; in the case of your own planning, you save money and pretty much hope for the best. The trip can be great, a bust, or somewhere in the middle. The choice is yours. Like they say on TV, "It's your money."

All of this sounds like I'm coming down on the side of the outfitter, and maybe I am. But the days are numbered when you can drive your car to a neighboring state, inspect a farm from the road, ask—and get—permission to hunt, and waltz out and shoot a few pheasants. If it happens at all any more, there is usually a little legal tender changing hands for the courtesy. As much as we'd like to believe in the good old days, when it comes to free and unfettered access to a stranger's land while carrying a shotgun, well, these days, hunting is getting to be business. When game has economic value in relation to its plenitude, then those who are the custodians of that plenitude have a vested interest in perpetuating it.

And I, for one, don't think that's necessarily a bad thing. Sure, I wish it weren't so. I wish you could still knock on doors, get permission, and have a fine day shooting a few birds undisturbed by crowds. I also wish they'd find a cure for cancer, that new Purdeys cost $400, and that Michelle Pfeiffer would call me and breathe heavily into the phone.

The future of hunting, for a vast number of urbanites in this country, is going to lie with commercial enterprise, be it a James Bay goose camp, a south Georgia quail plantation, a hacienda in Mexico accommodating the dove-shooting crowd, or a local shooting preserve catering to members only or the public. The trick is going to be in judging the value of the experience: What do you get for the money and time you spend?

In some cases, the outfitter can make the adventure as Spartan as you'd like; in other cases, it's more lavish than anything you've ever experienced. You'll probably pay accordingly. Some places and excursions are set up for experienced wingshooters, refined in their skills and tastes; others are intended for the twice-a-year corporate executive on a business getaway weekend with a few clients; still others get most of their business from the rank beginner who is still enthusiastic about slow birds, thin cover, and meat dogs. In all cases, the burden is on the customer—you—to assess conditions ahead of time so you'll know at least approximately what you're getting for your money.

Some places are very big on quality of shooting, leasing lands, managing habitat, presenting mostly wild birds or flight-conditioned supplements to wild stock. They will have knowledgeable guides and savvy, classy dogs—and a lot of them. The shooting will not be "close to wild," it will be wild. Other facilities will specialize in the creature comforts, with lavish food and lodging facilities and a number of other things to do, such as sporting clays or perhaps fishing.

Still many others pride themselves on being at the top of the heap in both the sport and elegance departments. But having the best of sport with the proper number of people to assist, birds as wild as possible, dogs impeccably trained, lodging and food lavish, and ambience just what you want is costly. This is why a driven shoot in Europe or the U.K. is so expensive: the birds, the beaters, the keepers, the pickers-up and their dogs, and transportation are not cheap. Now factor in a country estate and formal dinners, and you get the picture. As it is, most of these shoots, regardless of the sportsman's cost, barely turn a profit.

Likewise, a Southern plantation with mule-drawn wagon, outriders, dog handlers, guides, wild or nearly wild birds, and plush plantation house with white-coated attendants and first-class Southern cooking and hospitality is not likely to be cheap—and it won't be if it expects to stay in business long.

For a long time, I have been mystified by the things hunters react to economically. I'm not saying they are wrong, I just have a hard time figuring it out. For example, if a hunting license goes up two dollars, or the duck stamp goes up three, there always seems to be much rending of garments. Likewise if shotshells rise in price more than a few pennies. This is always accompanied by talk of the "good old days" and how "things used to be." (You remember those times: Kids died of measles…your teeth fell out at 45—you know.) The guy who will gripe about a dollar here and a dollar there when it comes to sport will climb into a 4×4 that cost what his house used to; he'll feed his bird dog hi-pro rations, spending a dollar a day during the season to do it; he'll go through $150 boots and $80 brush pants. But he'll not see the light for a couple dollars here and there for a license or a stamp.

A couple years ago, a duck-hunting friend of mine bought an expensive boat and trailer combination at about the same time the duck stamp went up $2.50 or $3, something like that. He was telling me that waterfowling had gotten so expensive, he should just quit. I told him the trailer hitch for his Jeep to pull the boat cost the equivalent of 25 years' worth of the $3 increase. He gave me the fish eyes. Have you ever noticed that some things with some people just don't *take*?

The point is that we often spend a lot of money on equipment because, in a very material way, these are assets. We then hesitate to spend the money necessary to go places and enjoy these things. An acquaintance of mine told me that, after years of buying, selling, and trading guns, he was through with it. He was going to keep the guns he had right this minute and spend the money he used to spend on guns to go places and use those guns.

And at the end of the day, isn't that what it's really about?

By the way, here's a tip: If you're over the magical age of 35, remember that no matter how keenly you anticipate a trip, the third day out is usually the worst. Normally, you're pretty well worn out by then from the trip and the nearly immediate exertion of hunting for two days. Experienced traveler-shooters often take that day off from hunting. See some sights, sleep in, poke around the countryside. What you do doesn't matter, just relax—all of this is supposed to be fun. This way, a full week out can be better enjoyed.

Anyone who thinks that hunting is going to become anything but more "elite" (a synonym to many for "it's going to cost more") is in for a rude awakening. This country is no different than any other where there is finite public land and a gang of us who want to use it. But what is the definition of elite, as used when it's tagged on upland bird or waterfowl hunters? Is it using a nice gun—a double that happens to be the most effective upland piece ever devised? Then we are guilty. Is being elite using a dog to help us and teaching the dog the right way to do things so that we neither waste game through crippling loss nor lose opportunities to bag game because the bird flushes them out of range? Is it elitist to quit shooting before you've reached the legal limit because, well, just because? Is it elitist to count crippled birds toward your limit? No—and in many states, it's the law.

Sportsmanship is neither a matter of the gun you carry nor the breed of dog that accompanies you. It is a code of conduct, a matter of appreciation expressed through actions consciously taken and many not taken in the field in pursuit of game. There are slobs who shoot Purdeys and real gentlemen and ladies toting 870s.

But I'm not going to kid you, my experience has been that the chances of seeing outrageous acts committed against sporting ethics and fair chase by a fellow with a fine English setter and a European double are pretty minimal. If this is stereotyping, so be it, and I'm not making any judgments against those who don't hunt this way. I'm just telling you what I've seen across all of North America in almost 40 years of chasing birds.

Using a fine shotgun of game gun persuasion to hunt birds is not a matter of elitism, it is the height of practicality. For one thing, a really good gun from London, Birmingham, Eibar, Gardone, or any other gunmaking center is built so that your great-grandson may have to replace a firing pin or have the locks checked. It is built to last forever, and if you don't believe by now that the best you can afford is nearly always a bargain, I'm not going to convince you in a few paragraphs.

Further, guns are made, or can be altered, to fit your shooting style, body conformation, the birds you most often hunt, even the shot charge you favor. Thus, you shoot as if the gun is the part of you with which you look at the pretty birdies. Take an old hand with a gun made for him who has shot it for years and is used to it, like the habits of an old friend, and I'll show you a man who has a clean left barrel and a comfortable bulge in his game bag. Does this make him an elitist or merely elevate him to the highest level of practicality?

Are these guns expensive? Of course. Are they expensive when compared with, say, a bass boat or a 4×4 vehicle, or two rounds of golf a week all summer for a couple of years? No, not really (okay, some are). It is a matter of where you want to place your loose change. I hunt with a fellow who shoots cheap guns and drives to coverts in a $36,000 Suburban hauling a pair of $4000 pointers. He has made his choice. I like to hunt with him because his ride is infinitely better than my six-year old Chevy pickup. He ribs me about the cash I spend on guns; I tell him he could put his dogs through Yale for what they cost him. We both like the paths we've chosen.

Finally, elitism can be defined as respect, an esteem for the rituals and traditions of hunting, the liturgy of wingshooting. It is respect for the birds, taken in fair chase, using tools that have, over the generations, proved themselves to be the ones most suited, practically and aesthetically, for the task at hand.

We all have run across those who have no seeming regard for the birds whose lives they take, nor the manner in which they pursue them. This manifests itself in a variety of ways—fixation on taking a limit, overbagging, trespassing, littering. It is the frontier mentality of conquest and moving on, of being out in nature without seeming appreciation of its fragility and our place in the scheme.

So if we are elite in our tastes and pursuits and the manner in which we have chosen to live our sporting lives, then we should plead guilty with alacrity. It is the highest compliment someone can give us.

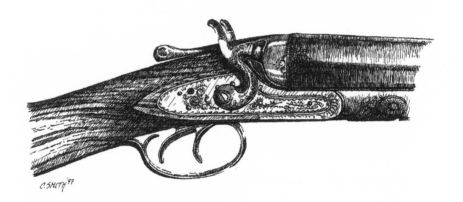

Technique

Shooting as Athletics: Part I

ISN'T IT INTERESTING THAT something as complicated as wingshooting is regarded as existing in a vacuum, apart from other eye-hand coordination activities?

Yet, those with even a smattering of athletic experience know that so many of the rules of athletics could be used to make us better shots —but first we have to look at things that way.

Take, for example, some of the precepts of other, familiar sports. What do golfers learn in just about the first minute of the first lesson? Well, it's the same thing baseball players learn and bowlers, and tennis players getting ready to serve, and basketball players getting ready to shoot free throws, and a dozen others sports you can name: proper stance and proper footwork.

In each case, if you'll refresh your memory, somebody giving instruction is going to say something like, "Make sure your weight is evenly distributed and don't rock back on your heels; keep your weight on the balls of your feet and your knees slightly flexed."

A shooting stance is no different—same advice. "Face the shot" goes along with this, because very often we incorrectly shoot with the left foot well forward of the right (for right-handers), the gun pointing forward laterally across the body. Not only does this stance not allow proper seating of the butt in your shoulder pocket—it ends up out on your arm instead—it also binds your swing up if the target cuts left. You won't be able to follow.

Also, fearing recoil, some shooters, especially beginners, lean back on their heels. This binds up the swing, makes the head rise from the stock, and actually increases felt recoil because the head isn't in firm contact with the stock. This firmness is a requirement to keep from getting battered and to take advantage of gun fit. Would you rather that George Foreman put his fist on your shoulder firmly and then pushed, or placed his fist two inches away and then punched? The push is felt, but with no pain; the punch hurts. When you hold your face away from the stock, it gets a running start at your cheek, resulting in a punch, not a push.

In addition, if you want a gun to shoot where you look, you must hold it as nearly the same way each time as you can. Lifting the head a little bit one time, a lot the next, and not at all the next will never give you the consistency you need to be anything more than an average shot. Watch a first-class shot. His head position, like his foot position, is always the same. He may not grind his face down on the stock like he's trying to wear it out, but his face will always have contact with the stock in exactly the same way, shot after shot after shot. To the bowhunter or target archer, coming to the same point in the draw of the bowstring every time is called the "anchor point." The face on the stock is the shotgunner's anchor point.

And what do other sports teach us about head position and keeping our head motionless? Golf? Hitting a baseball? The approach in bowling? Keep your head still; there's less chance your eyes will play tricks on you if their container—your head—isn't bouncing around.

Back to footwork. You are facing the shot; that is, your feet are almost on the same plane shoulder-width apart, the left advanced an inch or two, and weight on the balls of the feet, the knees flexed. You find you can swing the gun easily to the left. However, you can also swing to the right by pivoting, feet in place, so that the majority of your weight shifts to the right foot. For all the world, it is exactly the turn a right-handed golfer makes when taking the club back during his backswing. You can shoot nearly behind you this way without repositioning your feet. Not only is it stable, it's also faster, especially in thick cover, than trying to actually step so you're facing right. Try it.

And as far as making a shot to the left, the pivot in that direction is exactly like the position you would assume in the follow-through after hitting a full golf shot: weight on the left foot, the right foot bearing a little weight and perhaps up on your toe, the hips square to the target as much as possible. When your hips face the target, so do your shoulders, and therefore the gun will be more accurately pointed by the whole body, not just the hands.

Let's stay with golf since so many of the movements and precepts are the same with shotgunning and golf. Let's see: stance, weight distribution, swing to the right, swing to the left, keep your head still.

What about follow-through? We know that any sport requires it, especially those using an object or tool—a golf club, a baseball bat, a tennis racquet, a ping-pong paddle, a bowling ball, a hockey stick, and so forth. The reason for follow-through, carrying the action beyond the point of its completion, is because if you don't, you'll stop somewhere short of completion.

Try this: Swing a tennis racquet at an approaching ball hard enough to return it over the net, but do so with the idea that you will stop the racquet immediately after hitting the ball. You will start to slow your swing before you make contact with the ball, and you'll miss, mis-hit, or not hit it hard enough to return the shot. In other words, you'll hit a poor shot. You are anticipating and preparing for the *stop*, not the *shot*. You miss, I win. You buy the drinks.

How about golf, again? Take putting, the most demanding part of the game to those who have to "...putt for dough." Try lining up a long putt—say, 20 to 25 feet, and again tell yourself you are going to hit the putt hard enough to get it to the hole, but you'll stop the putter head as soon as you're sure you've made solid contact. Shouldn't be a problem, right? The ball should already be on its way to the hole by the time you stop your swing. What difference does it make to the golf ball if you have stopped your swing after you've already struck the putt? Well, it does. You will hit either too short, too long, right or left, but you won't make it very often, not compared with the longer, follow-through style of putting that professionals teach in which the putter head follows for 18 inches to two feet along the target line after the putt is struck. The reason? If you try to stop the putter too soon after the putt is struck, you'll stop it before it's struck.

Now, let's take shooting. A bird flushes and crosses left to right. You have the right stance, the right swing, the right gun, the right choke. You mount, catch the bird, overtake, and fire when the muzzles pass the bird. But he keeps going, and you see twigs fly off a tree directly behind him.

How could you have been behind like that? Because you were so interested in making the shot, in seeing its effect—it's fun to watch the bird drop—that you slowed down the swing in anticipation of stopping it. Why use all that extra effort? I was ahead of the bird when I fired! Were not. You were when you started to fire, but by the time your eye communicated with your brain that things looked right, your brain processed the information and passed it along to the motor muscles in your trigger hand via your spinal cord, you had slowed down—just enough to be behind. Don't even try to factor in that, because of not practicing lately, maybe your eye was a little wrong to start with, or the trigger pulls weren't right so the lock time was slower than you'd like, or you had a fight with your wife and were thinking about things like community property. Just consider follow-through here.

In effect, you must make yourself swing the gun until the bird is hit or a miss is certain. That's the reason for the long, exaggerated swings by championship skeet shooters on crossing targets: It's the only way to be entirely sure that a miss is not caused by swing-stoppage.

The world of sports is full of references to momentum, most of them alluding to a team on a winning streak or an individual athlete having a good year. But momentum in the sense of physics is also important, especially to swing and follow-through.

A golf club, in order to generate the power needed to hit a ball properly, is started well back and brought through the hitting zone at speed. Ditto for a tennis racquet, baseball bat, hockey stick, etc. If speed is adequate, follow-through is sort of automatic—the tool, once started, cannot be instantly stopped. But if it starts out too slowly, it lacks the necessary momentum to help carry it along and through its path.

Now, take a shotgun. If you mount the gun, find the bird, and then start swinging along the bird's flight, the gun will not consistently achieve the necessary momentum to aid in follow-through. Golfers know that one of the toughest shots is the little "touch" chip around the green. Because the shot has to be hit softly, the Sunday golfer tries to do it with a lazy swing, stopping the lazy swing prematurely, and duffing the shot. The pro golfer uses a shorter backswing, a faster stroke, and a longer follow-through. He gets paid a whole lot of money for doing it because he does it right.

If we take time to see the bird, to pivot the body along its line of flight as the gun is coming up, we have started to give the gun the necessary momentum to complete follow-through even before it reaches the face.

Further, to make sure we don't dawdle and stop the swing, the shot should be triggered as soon as the face is at its anchor point on the stock. In other words, the swing actually takes place as the gun is coming up, the shot just after it's mounted. Follow-through is then automatic, like a baseball hitter, who starts his swing with the bat out of his view (gun-mount), brings it into the hitting zone to meet the ball (cheeking the stock), makes contact with the ball (the shot), and follows through (follow-through).

Along with follow-through, you must also be decisive. You can't be tentative and be a good shot consistently, because, again, things get out of whack and you'll do something wrong—lift your face, stop your swing, slow your pivot, etc. This advice also has its basis in other sports. The golfer who decides where and how hard to hit the ball does it best when he just goes ahead and hits it. You can't really "sort of" hit a hard volley over the tennis net. Speaking of which, have you ever seen a professional tennis player try a short little dink shot barely over the net as his opponent was in the back court, and he skulls it into the net instead? Too tentative. What about the basketball player on a breakaway who tries a finger-roll layup instead of a dunk and the ball bounces…bounces…and bounces away? They weren't going for it —they were hoping.

The shooter has to realize that he too must go for it, must be aggressive, must be decisive. And the best way to do that is, once you have decided to shoot, shoot! Again, as I said before, shoot as soon as the gun is mounted. Don't track the bird, don't dwell on the target, don't get the equivalent of the putting yips and freeze. Do like the baseball player: Make sure you see clearly what you're going after, watch its flight path and direction, make up your mind when and where to hit (shoot), and then do it without hesitation. Humans as a collection of loose parts actually function pretty well that way—they use their instinctive reactions the best.

Shooting As Athletics: Part II

WE THINK NOTHING OF GETTING a bowling ball drilled or the shaft stiffness on our golf clubs checked. Baseball bats come in various lengths, weights, barrel diameters, and grip sizes—whatever fits you. Tennis racquets have grip size differentials to account for differences in hand sizes among users. A hockey player will choose a stick with just the right curve at the business end, and there's a cottage industry in this country that makes custom pool cues.

But citizens who wouldn't think of walking up to the house ball rack at bowling lanes and using the first ball they grab, will do just that with a shotgun, claiming that it feels okay and besides, fit is overrated. But aside from golfers, who will go to the time and trouble of having their swing analyzed and clubs chosen to accommodate that swing, the rest of the sports world sort of goes by feel, just as shooters do.

The trouble with that is that just because a gun feels right doesn't necessarily mean it shoots right. There is the "showroom fit," that great feeling a fine gun gives us in the gunroom, and there's the "field fit," how fit stands up under the rigors and excitement of shooting.

For example, years ago I had a gun with a great fit job—in the stocker's shop. It was only after I started shooting the gun (poorly) and was out with a knowledgeable friend at a sporting clays course that the truth came winging home.

"Do you always shoot with your mouth ajar?" he asked.

"I never do," I answered.

"Five bucks you do," says he.

He was right. In the unhurried shooting of plates and patterns and so forth during a fitting, I shoot with my mouth closed; in the excitement of the field, I shoot with my mouth ajar—for some reason. Anyway, if you put your stock to your face with your mouth closed, then open your mouth slightly, you will see the difference between showroom fit and field fit.

Strangely, one of the most ignored and overlooked aspects of learning to be an effective wingshooter as it relates to other sports is coaching.

We are a nation of athletes, people who play amateur sports well into middle age and beyond and who hold professional athletes out as icons. And at every single level, from Casey Stengel to Bear Bryant to Vince Lombardi, we have canonized and held in the highest esteem the role of coaches. From the lowliest little league coach to the highest levels of professional competition, coaches contribute to the learning of athletes.

In every major metro area of the country, you can find golf professionals, tennis pros, even aerobics instructors. But for some reason, shooters don't find it within their realm of experience to employ a coach either as a corrector of accrued faults or as teacher to a beginner.

Maybe since hunting is, perfectly, both relatively solitary and non-competitive, we think of coaches as those who help us win, who assist us in bettering the competition. And the competitive aspects of shooting in the field either do not exist or are often not acknowledged or discussed.

But they are there nonetheless. If you are honest, you would admit that it wouldn't be too much fun to go out with a buddy, watch him drop his three roosters with three right barrels, and then follow you around for the rest of the day while you go oh-for-Saturday. It isn't that we are necessarily competing with him, but it is nice to hold up our end of things. In England, where shooting was, and to a certain extent still is, a social event, shooting poorly is something of an error among certain classes. Where game harvested is considered a crop—a cash crop—and where an estate owner pays dearly for birds, game-keepers, beaters, pickers-up, lunches in the field, and formal dinners, there is very little that is charmingly delightful about a shooter who will stand there and miss 50 driven pheasants speeding overhead. A poor shot, there and then, is a liability. He wants a good bag, the gamekeeper wants a good bag, and the other guests do as well.

So, for years Brits have employed shooting coaches who instruct new shooters, who sharpen the eye of an experienced shot, and who work on correcting faults that have a way of creeping up on us. They view the shooting coach exactly the way we here view the golf pro—as someone who can help us. They are not too proud, they don't think they are all related to Dan'l Boone, and they realize an hour with a good coach can do more to improve their shooting than several cases of shells.

The British coach, you should be warned, has a way of teaching that is instructive but quite regimented. Golf, for example, is a standardized sport. A golf pro once told me, "We know how to properly hit a golf ball; nobody is going to invent a new way. We just teach everyone the same type of swing."

But shooting, to my mind, is more like hitting a baseball. In all the major ways, a player's stance, grip, and swing are based in fundamentals. But there is room for variety. If you watch a golf tournament and then switch to a baseball game, you'll see that touring golfers all have swings very much like one another. But over on the baseball channel, major leaguers show much more individuality. I think shooting, in this regard, is more like baseball, allowing for personal adjustments. The golf instructor would like to build an automaton out of each and every pupil, getting him to turn his hips at the same time, grip exactly the same way, and so forth. The baseball coach allows for differences in build, reflexes, nervousness, and so forth.

Unfortunately, some British-style coaches subscribe to the golf-pro school of coaching, attempting to make their students all shoot the same. For a beginner, this is easy—he knows no other way. But for an experienced shooter, particularly an experienced American who has enjoyed a lot of success with a shotgun and just wants his style tweaked a bit, this can range from annoying to baffling, and he may get very little from the lesson. If he has always been a good shot, shooting with his left foot well-advanced, as most Americans do, and is instructed to "face the shot" and then does so and misses, there's a likelihood that he won't see where this fabled English style he's heard so much about is helping him. And he'd be right.

Good coaching means a shooter must have the experience necessary to take into account the individuality of his students and adjust for them. He should ask about your style of shooting, the game you hunt, the clothing you wear. He should be able to take into account age, eyesight, experience, the whimsical nature of varying reaction times from student to student, and so forth. In other words, a good coach should be able to take the student as he is and make adjustments in his style so that he improves, not force him to accept at face value a static formula for shooting. In this way, the shooting coach is more like the baseball coach than a golf pro. Now, maybe I'm all wet, but I think it takes a few gray hairs in the old mustache to do this; a 22-year-old "shooting instructor" probably isn't going to tell you or me what we need to know to improve. He's only going to teach us what he knows—the formula that someone recently taught him.

But, if you are missing inexplicably, almost any coaching is better than none—your buddy looking over your shoulder aside. In truth, some of the most perplexing misses come from very good shots who have a hard time with a certain shot and miss it virtually every time. This is called the "expert's miss," because they will miss it exactly the same way every time.

Some years back, on a Mexican white-winged dove hunt, I was having a tough time with the incoming-at-an-angle bird—coming toward me but not directly, sort of slipping off to the side as it passed overhead. Since in a good year in Mexico, you can practice any shot you want over and over again, I did just that. I realized that I'd missed that shot for years—never made it once, in fact. Turns out I was forgetting about the sideslip; I was covering the bird ahead, but not allowing for the bird's lateral movement. Once I figured that out, I hit more than I missed (of those, anyway).

Why We Miss—At Least, Why I Do

IF YOU ASKED THE AVERAGE wingshooter why he just missed a shot, you'd most likely get a shrug of the shoulders, a few mumbled excuses, or maybe just a blank stare, the stare indicating, "If I knew the answer to that one, I wouldn't miss again, now would I?"

The old saying about a hit being history and a miss being a mystery isn't entirely without basis. And that's too bad, because like golf, which has much in common with wingshooting, we should be able to learn at least something from our "mysteries." The problem in comparing the two is that we can see where the golf ball is going and pretty much figure out what we did wrong—a slice means you came across the ball, outside-in; a worm-burner means you topped it. The shot charge is impossible for the shooter, at least, to see, although some shooting coaches can see it.

Everyone can have an occasional bad day, but when things start stretching out into a bad season or a bad career, we have to evaluate what's going on and try to improve. One of the ways is to take stock of the situation and look at what's happening on both misses and hits to see what we can learn—from both success and failure.

For example, most misses seem to fall into certain categories:

Shooting Behind

Failure to lead the target enough and thus give the shot time to intercept a bird is the single biggest reason for a miss, most shotgunners would agree. This comes from not properly visualizing the shot string. On a crossing bird, the shot string can be like a sausage many feet long. If a bird comes in contact with that string at any point—sticks his head into it—he's in the bag. But let the string's front pass even one inch behind the bird, and it's a miss. Staying ahead of the bird is something of an act of faith, especially on long shots, where you must swing through and well ahead. "Keeping contact" with the target—that is, the muzzle close to the bird—feels comforting, but very often it results in misses because this contact results in less forward allowance than is needed. Starting the swing before the gun is mounted will generate the proper speed and momentum to allow the muzzle to pass through and ahead of the bird. Start by tracking the bird and, holding the gun with the stock tucked under the armpit and against the ribcage, swing along its path of flight, catching up to it. Then, still swinging, mount and fire as the muzzle passes the front of the target. With sufficient speed of swing, the long string will be thrown ahead of the bird, which will come in contact with some section of its length for a clean hit.

Shooting Over—Missing by Being Too High

This is the result of a couple of factors. The first is simply picking up your head to get a better view, the muzzle rises with your face, and you shoot over. Poor gun fit is usually a contributing factor, but a gun that shoots high is greatly desired over one that shoots low. Most experienced shotgunners prefer a high-shooting gun because they can hold a bit under the mark, see it clearly above the barrels, and hit. A low-shooting gun, especially on rising game, must be held so as to cover the bird in order to hit.

Too Fast/Too Slow

If you are so slow that the birds are paired off and nesting by the time you shoot, that's obviously not good. But what is meant here is being too deliberate and too precise, thus losing the essential momentum. This slowness most often results in misses behind as described above. A shotgun is not a precise weapon—it's for pointing, not aiming. Shoot as the butt nestles into your shoulder pocket, otherwise you aim, slow down, start peeking, and the misses pile up.

Being too fast is just as bad. Often it results in misses because the shot is taken without proper technique and mounting. Very often the closeness means your pattern has had little chance to open up, increasing chances for a miss. Even if you hit, the bird is often rendered useless for the table—and that should bother you. Like golf, timing is important—the shooter, like the golfer, has to make haste slowly, each in his own natural rhythm so that there is adequate time to do what must be done in the time allotted, being neither too fast nor too slow. This varies with the individual; some folks are naturally fast, others not. But most people's speed is not related to things like fast-twitch muscle fiber or athletic ability; it has more to do with intensity. Athletes call it "concentration," but your speed can be increased if you concentrate, allowing your intensity to build for the task at hand.

One of the reasons that older shooters are often a bit slower is because the intensity is not what it once was; they've shot plenty of birds and another hit or miss will make little difference; they are out there for something different. But often, this decreased intensity makes them better shots, because they pass up the quick, marginal chance and wait for the sure thing. Left barrels very often come home clean.

Conversely, there is the ultra-intense shot, usually found in a bit younger or at least somewhat inexperienced shooter, who is determined to take at least his share of the shots. He goes through the field as if he's on patrol rather than hunting. Here, the intensity level is so high that the shooting is too fast and misses result. For this person, realizing that there is more to hunting and shooting than the total bag ultimately will make him or her a better wingshooter, but this usually takes time. One thing that will often slow this shooter down is hunting alone. The excessive speed often comes from an unrecognized competitive situation with a shooting partner. When he hunts alone, such an individual is sure any shots taken will be his alone and he can slow down, be smoother, stop rushing, and enjoy the whole thing.

The Wrong Gun

Again, like golf, the tool has to be right for the job. Rarely does an opportunity present itself to hit a 40-yard pitch-and-run with a 3-wood. Likewise, even the best shot can be handicapped with a 30-inch, full-choked 12-gauge pump in woodcock coverts. Here, of course, is where the fun starts—the reading, the shopping, the buying and selling and trading to get just the right bag of clubs (battery of shotguns) for the jobs you most often ask them to do. And if there is a perfect gun for any shooting condition, every day, in all weather and in any habitat, none of us has met it yet.

Here's something else to think about: For the average right-handed shooter, a crossing shot headed right to left is easier than left to right. Why? Because in the former, the stock is coming into your face so your cheek stays down; in left to rights, the stock can easily be pulled away from your face, the barrels will drop, and you'll miss by shooting under. On those shots, you have to be sure to pivot your whole body. On right-to-left crossers, you can still make a fair number of them by being an arm-swinger. When I duck hunt, I always try to get the left side of the duck blind, because then most of the crossing shots are right to lefts; the left to rights are headed toward my partner, and those are his shots—and he's welcome to them. In a duck blind where you're seated, a full pivot is usually impossible.

By the way, if you're upland hunting, take the left side, again for the easier shot. Reverse everything I've said if you're left-handed. All of this, of course, is a form of cheating. You're welcome.

Making Doubles

THERE HE IS, AS SOLID as the brass cannon on the lawn of the VFW lodge. You had a hard time finding him in the Nebraska plum thicket, so he's been on point maybe three full minutes—a lifetime when you're looking for your dog and you know he's pointing quail.

You see him walleye you, rolling his eyes toward you and then back at the grass in front of him. His mouth is closed; he's taking all his air in through his nose, along with what must be the exquisite scent of quail—a covey of bobwhites that always works this side of the draw about this time of day.

You've spent hours and days and weeks and months training him. He quarters his ground, adjusts his range to the cover, checks in with you like clockwork, points and backs dead-solid, and retrieves like he should be spending his days in the duck blind. He's the best dog you've ever had, the one all your other, yet-unborn, dogs will be compared with years after he's gone.

And right now, he's got this covey staked cold. Now, it's your turn.

You come in from the side, pinching the birds away from the cover, trying to push them toward the open, trying to give yourself a clear shot. Your approach is quick but controlled, your gun at the ready. You kick the grass, and a dozen birds boil out, buzzing away. You pick a bird, swing through, and fire. He puffs. Another catches your eye and you go after him, but he cuts away from the open into the cover and he's gone. No other birds remain, so you release the dog with, "Hunt dead," reload, and congratulate yourself on a good shot.

But boy, it sure would have been nice to make a double. Especially for him. Just as a dog as broke as he is can do it all, you should, as the shooter, be able to do it all when you have the chance. And in upland bird fields and coverts, doing it all with a shotgun means making doubles. Is there anything better than a cracking point, quick birds, and a snappy right and left, two dead in the air? Not all the time, of course, and it's okay to miss a few now and then, but it sure would be nice, once in awhile, to pull it off.

So, why do so few gunners do it—make doubles? There are probably a lot of reasons, some mental and some physical. Like all acts of eye-hand coordination, it requires proper mechanics and discipline. But for a good shot who has never made many doubles, the mental part of the game has to be overcome first.

You have to put yourself in the mindset of shooting two birds. Quail, of course, present the best, most consistent opportunities for true doubles, and here is an aside on what makes a true double:

1. Both birds have to be in the air before the first shot is fired, otherwise, they are staggered singles, memorable, but not a double;
2. You must take the two birds with two shots, meaning two birds down with three shots from a repeating gun allows you to say, "I got two," but you can't say, "I got a double."

Next, and perhaps more importantly, you must make sure this does not detract from the aura of hunting and become a goal onto itself lest it trivialize the act of shooting a sporting bird into a target game. But that is the choice of each person. For one to say, "I would never shoot a double because it demeans the bird" is but a short step from saying, "I would never shoot a single because it demeans the bird." We are, after all, out there with a shotgun.

Now, the mental part of the game. First, like achieving anything in sport, you must first give yourself a chance to be in a situation where you can achieve the goal. If you golf, you know you can't win a two-dollar Nassau by knocking the ball out of bounds right away—you've got to start off in the fairway. So it is with shooting: You must give yourself a chance to make doubles.

Part of this chance comes, naturally, with the right gun and all that goes with it: choke, shot size, stock fit, barrel length, weight, balance, and all the rest. Even though the gun is part of the mechanical function, it is also part of the mental game, because if you have confidence in your shotgun, you'll shoot it better, freeing you to be more aware of the other things you have to do.

You must position yourself so that you will have the best chance to shoot. With quail, for example, most shots come as the birds fly toward cover. Positioning yourself so that birds fly dead away from you toward cover will give you straightaway shots, the easiest to make. In the example I gave above, the shooter tried to push birds toward the open, away from their natural flight path when close to cover. They flushed and then cut back, offering a chance for only one bird. Ruffed grouse, likewise, fly for cover, while such birds as woodcock often fly toward daylight. Being aware of the likely flight pattern before it happens helps.

Next, you must shoot the first bird before you can shoot the second. My observation is that the bird most often missed on an attempted double is the first bird because the shooter is doing what athletes so often do—he's trying to do the second thing before he does the first. Like the golfer who looks up from a putt before it is struck, a shortstop who tries to throw before he has the ball, or an NFL flanker who turns to run upfield before he has safely caught the pass, the shooter who is looking for a second bird before shooting the first will normally hit neither.

You must see a bird, pick it out, and shoot it. In the case of quail, Huns, and other covey birds, you must shoot one of the first birds off the ground, meaning when you do shoot, there will be other, closer birds flitting across your vision and field of fire. You have to ignore these and shoot the farther bird. When you do, the birds that were close will now be out there, at about the same range your first bird was when you shot it. If you shoot a close-in bird first, ignoring the farther birds, by the time you get around to shooting the second half of your double, they will all be out of range. No double. On quail, most successful doubles find the birds on the ground very close to one another.

They are also close to one another laterally, too, because the best way to shoot a double is to pick two birds taking the same flight path in the same direction. Rarely will you ever shoot a bird, spin 180 degrees, and shoot the second. In most cases, this means straightaway birds, but in other cases, crossing shots offer the best chance for a double. If you are hunting with a partner and a covey flushes, make sure you take birds only on your side. This is not only the most sporting way, it also increases your chances of a double because your part of the covey is smaller, the available target area more restricted, and the birds in that section are likely to be flying in the same direction.

Let's say you are at the end of a Kansas fencerow, blocking. Your partner is coming toward you with the dogs. Ahead of them, a pair of rooster pheasants flushes wild, curving with the prairie wind, one behind the other, 15 feet apart. They will pass you at 30 yards, crossing right to left. You immediately start thinking double. Now, there is neither a farther nor a closer bird, so the way to handle this is to mount and swing, catch up with the rear bird, fire, and continue your swing past the front bird and fire. If you shoot the front bird first, you'll have to stop your swing, wait for the back bird, and start again…and mostly, you'll miss.

Other aspects of making doubles have to do with just good wing-shooting technique and form: proper footwork, good gun mount, smoothness, follow-through, and so on. Naturally, readiness and concentration are paramount.

Competition with other shooters can affect some people. Some gunners rise to the challenge and shoot better; others choke and do worse. Just as in any athletic endeavor, there are clutch hitters and those who fade under the pressure. Dave Meisner and I often hunt together, and we always have the traditional three-dollar bet on best shooting average. I can't speak for Meisner because he always shoots well, to hear him tell it, but I know I'm a better shot when big bucks like that are on the line.

Finally, you have to realize that there are some birds on which you will perhaps never make doubles, even though opportunities can be legion. The best example of this would be brush-country quail. A covey of Texas bobwhites coming off the ground in cactus patches will offer very limited target selection, and you have to take what you can get. Be content with a single bird.

Other birds will just *never* give you an opportunity because they are solitary dwellers and if they are in the air together, it's a coincidence. For example, I have never shot a true double on woodcock, even though they are my favorite bird and at least half my hours afield over the last 35 years have been spent chasing them. I have shot staggered singles more times than I can count, but never a true double. I have had two bona fide chances for a woodcock double, and blew both—the last time, I missed everything. Others tell me about all the doubles they've shot on woodcock. They claim they aren't shooting staggered singles.

I think they're lying to me.

The Tough Angles

THERE ARE A CERTAIN NUMBER of shots that baffle all of us. As someone who is baffled by the angles birds can present and, by actual tabulation, has missed every legal species of upland bird in North America, I'd like to give you a bit of advice on some of the hard angles and tough shots some birds can present. Maybe it'll help you do a little better this year. These are just some odds and ends, but ones you can practice at your local sporting clays course. Let me emphasize that I don't make these any better than anybody else, proving again that most of us know how to shoot better than we actually do.

Incoming Doves

I don't know about you, but for me, the toughest shot on doves is the true incomer, the one that passes directly overhead, especially with a tailwind, as if a dove needs a tailwind. The right way to make this one is to swing from behind, catch up and pass the bird, blotting it out. Problem is, most of us peek. Since the only way to peek is on one side of the gun or the other, that means we end up shooting to the side and missing. Try to remember that if the lead and follow-through felt right on a high incomer (including driven birds and incoming clays), you probably missed because you peeked to the side. Of course, it's still possible to shoot behind on doves, and most of us do. But we tend to know it when we do it. Being aware of miss-by-peek helps you with the seemingly unexplainable misses.

Prairie Birds

Birds like Hungarian partridge and sharptails, which go up in coveys in the wide-open spaces, seem to always have a tail-end Charlie waiting in the grass until I empty my gun at the first ones off the ground. When this one takes wing, I'm usually standing there with a harmless hunk of steel and walnut. If you aren't in a good position to take a bird on the initial rise, don't shoot. Instead, hustle over to where the birds flushed and be ready. Very often, these are the easiest shots you'll get all day. Knowledge of a bird's habits can help you shoot better.

Close-in Pheasants

If there is a more embarrassing miss than a rooster pheasant at 12 yards, I haven't done it (except for a decoying Canada at 10). The bird is the size of a kite, and you ought to be able to hit him with a slingshot. But because he seems so easy, we get careless and sort of throw the shot out there, and too often we miss.

If you find this happening, try to shoot a part of the bird. With pheasants, it pays to be as head-conscious as it does with waterfowl. Try to see the head as the target and concentrate on shooting it. Also, bear in mind that many of us are overchoked for such shots. You should—rightfully—be using a lot of choke for pheasants. They are tough birds requiring multiple hits of big shot. But often the average shot is 30 to 35 yards, where modified on pheasants is right. The 10-yard shot, then, gives you the handicap of a tight choke coupled with the above-mentioned carelessness. So, c-o-n-c-e-n-t-r-a-t-e. Of course with tight chokes, there's no rule that says you can't wait for a bird to get out a bit before you shoot.

Incoming Geese

These birds are difficult because they are deceptive. A goose with its wings set, dropping into your decoy spread in an open field, is moving faster than it seems and dropping faster than it appears. Multiply the bird by maybe a dozen to 20 others, let panic set in, and you have the makings of a two-barrel, sucker-shot miss, the kind where you just stand there with your mouth open wondering how.

Incoming geese have to be led ahead and below. Once you shoot, they will start to fight for elevation, and they will rise as fast as a flushed woodcock heading for forest canopy. Then, we have to hold above them. They are also flaring, usually backward, so that has to be taken into account. Most misses on decoying geese come from shooting over as they're coming in and under as they leave.

Tough Crossers

This one isn't limited to any one bird, because all of them offer us crossing shots. If you are right-handed, the easiest crosser is right to left, for most of us. This is because the gun is coming into your face. On a left-to-right shot, the gun is being pulled away from the face, and you have to really pivot to keep up with it. If you make the right to left shot but consistently miss the left to right, try staying loose, pivoting, and making sure your face keeps firm contact with the stock.

Of course, "tough" crossers really translates into "long and fast" crossers, because of the need for greater lead in order to connect. Swinging through the target is the best way, of course, but if the shot is in the 40-yard range, try swinging through and seeing a bit more daylight before you shoot. In effect, swing through a "moving spot" that is ahead of the bird a foot or so. Imagine the bird with a vapor trail behind and spot a foot in front. Swing along the vapor trail and shoot when the muzzles pass the spot. And keep swinging. More on the "moving spot" later.

Most of the time that's about the best advice I can give you: Just keep swinging.

Seeing the Muzzles...and the Rib and the Bead and Everything Else...

HERE'S A COUPLE OF INCIDENTS from last season. The first took place in the ruffed grouse covers of Michigan. Our Lab, Maggie, was working scent (yeah, I very often hunt grouse with a Lab; so what?) in a thick alder patch. I was walking a trail about 10-feet wide on the edge, listening to the dog snuffle and crash about in the thick stuff. (See why the Lab? She goes in there and flushes, I stand outside and shoot at whatever she rousts out. Sometimes.)

I heard a grouse fight the branches as he launched ahead of Maggie. The bird, a gray phase bird-of-the-year, crossed the path left to right, not quite at full steam, but getting there. I snapped up my 20-gauge grouse gun, 26-inch barrels bored IC/M, and yanked a shot off, swinging as fast as I could, totally unaware of the gun. A globe of feathers hung suspended in the air at the extreme right edge of the trail. Maggie made the retrieve to hand. Heh, heh, heh.

A couple of months later, toward the tag end of the season, I was hunting pheasants in Iowa with Dave Meisner and his crackerjack little Elhew pointer, Gilly.

We were working into a lusty wind, and Gilly caught scent near a farm trail. Head high, Gilly worked the running bird up a fencerow until he pinned it solidly in a clump of wild plum just before the cover thinned to bare ground. Dave, to my left 50 yards, waved at me to move in, and as I did, the bird flushed, towering, a big rooster with a tail like a kite. He turned with the wind and started back over my head, toward the thick cover of a riverbed a quarter-mile behind us. I tracked him with the same little sidelock 20 I often use on grouse, but with the second set of barrels in place—28 inches bored M/F. As the muzzles passed the bird's head, I hit the front trigger and he went limp.

The wind carried him down the fencerow behind me, where he bounced hard. Gilly hopped the old wire and made a nice retrieve over to Dave. He glanced at the bird and called over, "Where'd you hit?"

It's a little game Meisner and I play. We call it, "Where'd You Hit?" It goes along with the other games we play—three bucks on the first bird and two bucks in the kitty for every shell missed. At the end of the season, we take the kitty and do something fun with it. Some years I shoot so lousy, we could take the kitty and go to Bermuda.

I hollered back, "Should be in the head, right side." I could see Dave grin before he called back, "Your ability to make a lucky shot is exceeded only by your ability to make a lucky guess." I don't do things nearly that well nearly often enough, which is why I remember it.

The obvious lesson here is that with pheasants, a good dog and shooting for the front of the bird saves a lot of running after cripples or birds that are ultimately lost. You've read it and heard it a zillion times: Shoot for the white ring... The head is your target... You have to be head-conscious with pheasants... Hit him hard and quick or you won't get him. Well, it's all true.

You'll notice, I hope, that something else happened here, and this is what I'd like to examine. I mentioned that, "As the muzzles passed his head..."

How often do we read that? How often do we read and hear something like, "I swung through until a saw a little daylight ahead of the bird and fired." Or, as the British say, the proper swing-through technique consists of, "Butt, belly, beak, bang."

Then, we also hear presented as gospel something like the fact that you should never see the muzzles or the barrels, instead concentrating on the bird. And for the most part, we do. Every season, we pull off shots in which we have no earthly idea that there are barrels out there at all. Mostly, these are the quick shots in thick cover where there's no time to do anything except see the bird, mount, and fire.

But in many cases, we have the time and, in fact, do see the barrels or the muzzles. We compute lead, using as a reference point the barrels moving ahead of the bird.

To say on the one hand that a proper swing-through shot consists of starting behind the bird, passing it, and firing as the muzzle pulls ahead of the bird is fine. To then state in the next breath that you should do this without seeing or being aware of the muzzles makes little sense. How ya 'sposta know?

The answer is, of course, that most of us do see the barrels and even quickly compute lead as we are swinging, especially in crossing shots in the open: doves, most waterfowl, driven birds, maybe sharptails and Huns on the prairie. In close-quarters, where snapshooting is the rule, you'll rarely see the barrels. A lot of the time, you barely see the bird.

There's nothing wrong with this. It is a poor NFL quarterback who can only throw one type of pass. He'll float it when he has to, loft it long on the next play, and drill it over the middle the next time. The same goes for the various shots and clubs in golf. A tennis player may lob a shot, and then drive the next one to the baseline. So it is with shooting. One time you have to mount and fire in one motion, the next time may be a high crosser with several seconds of time to make the proper shot.

Certainly, you shouldn't focus on the barrels, looking at them instead of the bird—the bird should always be the center of attention. But you do see the barrels out there, out of focus, perhaps, but they are there as a visual reference to where the gun is pointing.

Robert Churchill, the famed shooting coach and gunmaker who expounded on the idea that a shooter should never see his barrels, points out in his book, *Game Shooting*, that one fine shot he knew used a very large front bead because a small bead wasn't as good a visual reference point for him. Churchill found no fault with the man's reasoning.

Strangely, getting older has an effect on how much you see the barrels. Young shooters have eyes capable of amazing (to guys my age) depth-of-field, capable of focusing on muzzles 35 inches away and a bird 35 yards away at the same time. As we get older and find the print on pill bottles getting smaller, it is only natural for us to see the bird clearly and the muzzles fuzzy and out-of focus. Much of what has been written about seeing the bird clearly and the muzzles not at all has been written by middle-aged shooters for whom it is impossible to do otherwise. In fact, being overly muzzle-conscious is a malady that plagues the old more than the young because the eyes found under graying brows take a discernible period of time to focus on the bird, then the barrel, then the bird again. Young eyes do it instantly.

So, if you're seeing the barrels on some shots and are even consciously computing lead, don't worry about it. There are a lot of us doing the very same thing.

Driven Pheasants

DRIVEN BIRDS—THE QUEEN MOTHER of wingshooting. If we can agree that nothing matches the pomp and ceremony and tradition of red grouse in the Scottish heather on the glorious Twelfth of August, we ought to be able to also agree that driven pheasants are at least the Lady in Waiting.

Not many of us will ever get to Scotland to shoot driven pheasants. But they are shot elsewhere—to the south in England, they are the mainstay, the bread-and-butter bird for syndicate shoots; they are shot in Europe on both sides of what was once the Iron Curtain; and, increasingly, they are being shot in this country at both private and open-to-the-public sporting clubs. In those instances, rather than birds being driven into the air over shooters (the "guns"), they are released from a high point of land or even a tower (hence the "tower shoot"). In any event, when they pass over the line of guns, they are usually high and carrying the well-known mail. Behind the guns, no matter where you go to shoot driven pheasants, there are dog handlers with their furry buddies ready to do the retrieving.

Driven shoots involve a great deal of ritual. There is a drawing for position, or "peg," the rotation of position after each drive, and there is a level of politeness that must be observed to make the shoot enjoyable for everyone. The first rule, of course, is safety: Shoot only at high birds in front of your station, and no turning to shoot behind. There are people to the right, people to the left, and people behind. In addition, whether it is beaters or releasers, there are people ahead somewhere, but out of range. In the case of the beaters, shooting will be halted before they get too close. If you break the rules even once, you will be asked to unload your gun and leave the premises and be right smart about it.

The second rule is "poaching," or shooting at the birds that rightfully belong to the gun next to you. I've seen this take place on every driven shoot I've ever been on, and almost without exception, this is a sin of ignorance: The shooter just didn't know what were his birds and what were not.

Essentially, unless you are at either end of the line, you get to shoot at the birds passing through your 45-degree field of fire. Imagine a slice of pie, the point of which is where you are standing and the "crust" being the edge of your range. As a bird gets closer, the area where it is inside your legal field of fire gets progressively smaller. In a perfect world, the bird enters your vision at the extreme edge of your field of fire, out there on the crust of the pie. It flies directly toward you, down your field of fire, and directly overhead, at the pie slice's "point" where you're standing. If the bird does not enter your slice of the pie, it's not your bird; if it enters your slice too low, it's dangerous to shoot.

Sometimes—often, in fact—the bird flies parallel to the line, never passing over the line or attempting to do so. Then, it's your bird when it crosses through your field of fire. Once at a shoot, the gun on my right started shooting at birds that were quartering through my field of fire heading toward—but not yet into—his field of fire. After several such birds, all of which he missed because they were too far out, I pointed out to him that the birds were in front of me and not him, and if he wanted to shoot that badly, I'd trade places with him. The poor fellow turned red and stammered that he didn't realize what he was doing. I believed him and there was no problem. Thereafter, I let birds headed his way go through, and he had great sport. But he'd got the message as well.

Once you get the hang of it, driven birds are relatively easy marks. I can hear the howls now, but let me explain. First, you aren't walking where you have to stop, get your footing, and mount the gun. You already should have your foot area free of impedimenta, the gun should be at the ready but not mounted, and you can usually see the birds well (when you can't, well, that's when things get very testing).

Second, the birds are coming toward you, exposing the head, neck, and vitals, making killing shots easier. Finally, the angles, with variations, are all fairly uniform. If you shoot at birds only in your field of fire, there is little difference bird to bird in the shots they present. You can make some long runs.

You can also make some long runs of misses if you don't get things figured out. Driven shooting shows off the "expert's miss" better than anything else: You miss every single shot the same way every single time. This miss is so named because the good shooter has little variation in his gun mount and swing, so he is consistent in his shooting. And if he is consistently assessing the shot incorrectly, he will miss every time. The beginner hits some and misses some because he never does the same thing twice in a row. Whether he hits or misses, he doesn't know what he did or how he did it, so he continues to guess. Once an expert figures out the angle, he then runs off long strings of hits because it was his judgment—not his technique—that was faulty.

The true incoming shot is missed almost universally because the shooter peeks. To make this shot, you start from behind the bird, swing through—in this case upward—and fire when the bird is covered by the gun barrels. This is one of those rare shots where you shoot at a mark you can't see. If you can see the bird, easy to do if you're peeking and therefore picking up your head, then you're probably behind it.

Which brings up the final common miss on driven birds, the one where a bird looks like a straight incomer but it's not, but you treat it as such and you miss laterally. It's necessary to really watch a bird to gauge its flight path before you go after it. Then, when you do, you do so quickly and authoritatively. Like all wingshooting, if you dawdle, you'll likely miss. I have to remind myself to shoot when the bird is well out to give the pattern a chance to work. Also, when the bird is still 40 yards away, it doesn't seem to be moving as quickly, which it isn't, relative to me. If I let a driven cockbird get too close, though, practically overhead, that's a tough shot because the angle binds up my swing, and he's really moving.

When the birds are getting closer instead of farther away, experienced shots fire the tight barrel first and then the open barrel. Doubles, the fabled "two dead in the air at once," are made in the same way, taking the first bird well out and the second closer with an open choke.

Before you plunk down cash for a driven shoot in some exotic clime, it's best to practice on a clays tower where shots can be approximated. I've never seen a good clays tower shooter do too poorly on driven pheasants. My friend, Glenn Baker of Benton, Pennsylvania, runs a shooting school just such as this at his Woodcock Hill grounds to prepare shooters for their European experience. Glenn's a certified British shooting instructor (who also owns the English gun company, Thomas Bland & Sons), and he and his wife, Christa, book driven shoots on estates in her native England. They use the school to prepare their clients and others for the shooting and conduct expected of driven-bird shooters.

The standard gun for such shooting is, of course, the 12-gauge, either over-under or the more traditional side-by-side. Other gauges are allowed, normally, but challenging high ("tall") birds normally require a 12. And if you shoot where shotshells are supplied, you may have a real job on your hands trying to get anything else. The guns built for such shooting are stocked high and straight to allow for a little built-in lead to help with the shots you'll encounter. Some even have very deeply swamped ribs to assist you in shooting high.

Proof, once again, that our guns very often know how to shoot better than we do.

Going Light: Too Much of a Good Thing

USE CAUTION AS YOU whirl about through the marketplace looking for the ultimate in the ultralight shotgun. As the old saw goes, be careful what you ask for, you just might get it.

Ultralight shotguns are fine as far as they go; the problem is, they often go too far—too far in balance sacrificed for weight savings, too far in momentum forfeited for weight savings, too far in barrel lengths being shortened to the detriment of handling for the sake of weight savings.

A shotgun that is so light it feels toylike, regardless of gauge, is not the best choice for most people. Mounting a shotgun during a hunting situation when the adrenaline is up borders on the violent, and an ultra-light shotgun has a tendency to bounce about once mounted. A heavier shotgun comes up and stays put, once mounted, so the shot many times can be triggered instantly, rather than after the bouncing stops. I won't even go into the felt recoil a very light gun passes on to your central nervous system and all the bad things that can happen to your shooting because you know you're going to get rapped when you pull the trigger.

A few years ago, I was walking back from a morning duck hunt, a bag of decoys over my shoulder. Since it was still fairly early, I had my shotgun still loaded and was carrying it with the muzzle in the air, the butt resting on my hip. I thought that a late-rising mallard might flap by or something. A snipe flushed almost underfoot at the edge of a little cove in the lake I'd been hunting and cut along the shoreline, jinking and zigging as they do. I dropped the decoys, raised the gun, tracked the bird, and dropped it (surprising both of us). Since I had been watching my footing when the bird jumped, I knew exactly where he was when he flushed—two steps ahead of me. I walked to that spot and then paced off 12 long steps to where the bird lay in the grass next to the lake. Twelve yards.

Now since I am not asked to endorse anything, have nothing named after me (boots for example), and the only plaque I ever got was on my teeth, I won't tell you the make of gun I was using because if I spread around the fact that I used such-and-such make of shotgun, it would throw the maker's sales into a tailspin. Be content if I tell you the gun was a repeating shotgun of 8½ pounds with a 28-inch modified barrel, and I was shooting 3-inch magnums. Yet the quick little snipe went down but 12 yards away, and I felt I had all day at that.

Am I that quick a hand with a shotgun? Well, if I had been a gunfighter in the Old West, they would have started burying guys when Boot Hill was brand new "right next to Smith."

No, I think that when a bird is up, it's apparent that most shooters have, if anything, too much speed. They snap the gun up and crack off an ill-advised shot as soon as the butt is in the vicinity of the shoulder. An ultralight shotgun only exacerbates the problem by being bouncy as well.

What's too light? Depends upon you, of course, and if you're young or old, but on average (and would all of us who are "average" agree to meet someday in a phone booth and talk about it?), I'd say anything under 6¼ pounds for a 12-gauge, 6 pounds even for a 16, 5¾ pounds for a 20, and 5½ for a 28 is starting to get too light. If carrying a gun that weighs a bit more than this tires you out and you feel you will be too weary to make a shot when presented at the "end of a hard day" we hear so much about, sit down and rest. This is supposed to be fun; if you sit and rest and the gun still feels too heavy, maybe you shouldn't be out there at all. See your doctor.

Those ultralight guns are fun to polish and swing at imaginary grouse in front of the fireplace on winter evenings, but you'll shoot better with a heavier gun. Trust me.

Getting Older

PART OF LIFE IS GETTING older, which beats hell out of the alternative, which is to die young.

Part of getting older is the effect it has on the things we enjoy doing. Okay, so maybe you can't hit a major league fastball anymore. You probably never could. But if you belong to the fiftyish crowd who enjoys wingshooting, you should take some solace in the fact that this is one sport where the best is yet to come. Experience counts for a tremendous amount in shooting, and most shooters get better as they ease into middle age.

For one thing, we've seen it all before, and we know pretty much what to expect from the birds we've settled on as our favorites. For another, the almost recklessness of youth, where we need to shoot a bird six feet off the ground, has given way to sager judgment, where we wait, see, swing, and shoot.

But, some things do change, and for one thing, the guns we use and to a certain extent how we use them become increasingly important and—lucky for our gunsmiths—usually in need of some tinkering and tweaking. There are other things you can do, too, to give yourself back some of the advantages you feel—often wrongly—the years have stolen from you. Since the average age of the readers of this book is probably somewhere in the mid- to late forties, these may help:

- We can probably use a little more drop in the stock. As we age, shoulder joints, neck muscles, and all the connective tissue become a tad more stiff, less flexible. It becomes a bit harder to get down on a high stock like we once did. Now, it's not much; I take about one-eighth inch more drop than I did in my twenties now that I'm, uh, no longer in my twenties. A slightly shorter stock helps shouldering as well, and again, not much—maybe a half-inch.

- Most of us end up shooting better with lighter guns than we used to because of the fatigue factor. Where the exuberance of youth can often make you throw the gun away, we now have the sagacity to control a light gun better. At least that's the theory. And where a six-pound gun once felt light, nowadays it feels about right, what I've had to say about ultralight guns elsewhere in this book notwithstanding. I'll bet you don't exactly pick your wife up and swing her around like you used to, either, even if she hasn't gained an ounce since college. Weight is relative to your ability to handle it. Toward that end, a little off-season work with light free weights of 5 to 10 pounds will keep your arms, shoulders, and wrists in good shape.

- Longer barrels tend to smooth out swings that might be a little herky-jerky. This is not dependent upon age, by the way. I happen to feel that everyone would shoot better with barrels of 28 inches than they would with shorter ones.

- Get your eyes checked. The ability to focus on a bird or clay target as it streaks away from you—and remain focused—diminishes with age as the lenses of your eyes harden and become less flexible. You should be wearing shooting glasses anyway, so getting a weak prescription ground into them is no big deal. But you've got to know if and what, so get ye to the eye doc.

- While you're at it, the ears aren't what they used to be, either. I'm not sure what to do about that, except perhaps to be aware of it. You use your hearing so often in upland shooting for locating a bird on its initial flush, that when time starts to muffle it a tad, it's disconcerting. I suppose that if it gets bad enough we can wear a hearing aid. Sometimes just realizing it and using your eyes more, being alert, can compensate for diminished hearing.

- Spend more time handling and swinging your gun during the off-season. Muscle-memory is capricious, and it escapes us faster with age. The days of hauling a gun out of the cabinet and taking it to the field and dropping 12 doves with 14 shots are probably gone. You need to handle a gun regularly in order to keep your muscles attuned to the gun, the pivot, and the swing.

- Before you head into the field, loosen up, the same way you would before your morning run (ha!). Stretch, bend, and swing at the waist with your feet planted. If you don't and you pull a hamstring going over a blowdown, believe me, you won't care how long your gun barrels are—you're done for the season. Part of shooting well is being able to be out there to do it.

- Get in shape. Closely related to the above, spend a lot of time getting in shape. I use a treadmill every other day all year for the old ticker, but lately I have started to walk outside more often prior to the season. Since I have a couple of out-of-shape bird hunters at my place living out their present reincarnation as black Labs, they need the exercise, too, after spending the long winter snoozing on the couch and eating Oreo cookies. I find that getting my legs in shape makes those Western hillsides and Eastern grouse thickets a little easier to take—and enjoy.

- Wear looser/lighter clothing. One of the (myriad) criticisms I have of shooting clothing made for North American consumption is that the stuff fits too tight and is often too heavy. This has nothing to do with my burgeoning waistline, so it isn't sour grapes. I'm talking about stuff that's constructed wrong for doing anything except sitting with your feet propped up sucking on a sundowner and waxing lyrical about "the good life." Walking is out of the question.

  I recently bought a pair of brush pants from a very well-known sporting goods outlet. They were light and the nylon facing tough. But if I picked my foot up more than six inches off the floor, the rear seam of the pants was embedded in my backside. Without a doubt, the most uncomfortable pants made. So choose clothes that won't tire you out, that bend when you do, and give and flex in all the right spots. Okay, so maybe you don't look like a catalog model anymore, ready for a jolly good day afield, but you'll last longer wearing something else.

  The lightweight boots that are on the market now were made for our old ankles and insteps. Pick up a good catalog and look at the selection. It would be hard to go wrong; light footwear makes the miles shorter.

- Go to tighter chokes. There's more on this in another place in this book, but the truth is, you won't shoot as quickly as you used to, so that means tighter chokes. A half-second delay on a sharptail moving at 35 miles per hour comes out to an increase in range of 17 yards. That's the difference between loose IC and a tight modified. Are you a half-second slower than you were 25 years ago? Me too. Perhaps this isn't due to the physical so much as the psychological factor; the frenzy of youth and the need to shoot a lot of birds has subsided, or should have, and this takes an edge off the intensity.

The Moving Spot

LONG-RANGE SHOOTING, especially the kind encountered in water-fowl hunting, is usually the toughest for most shooters. If we practice little during the off-season, it's even worse. Especially hard is the dead crosser at 35 to 40 yards, at a right-angle to the shooter. The amount of forward allowance necessary to have the shot string intercept a bird is almost staggering if you were to figure it out on paper.

Ever since the first days of shooting at birds in flight, shotgunners have worked their way around this by swinging the gun and passing through the bird, then firing with the moving gun ahead of the bird. Otherwise, it's long computations, moving the gun ahead in a fixed manner, keeping it there in a sustained lead manner, and keeping the gun moving after the shot. Way too much stuff to dope out.

The fast swing-through works very well in short-range situations. For example, your dog points a single quail. You walk in and the bird pops out, headed left to right, quartering away from you. The range is in the 15- to 18-yard region. You start your mount and swing, swinging fast. You catch the bird from behind with the muzzles, and as you feel them get up toward the front end of the bird, you fire. The quail puffs. It felt as though you were pointing right at the bird's head when you fired, but logic and physics have taught us we had to be ahead or the shot string would have passed harmlessly behind.

The momentum generated by your fast swing carries the muzzle past the bird as your brain tells you to shoot. This message is translated into action, passing from your brain down your spinal column to your finger on the trigger. The finger trips the trigger, allowing the hammer to fall, which then strikes a firing pin that detonates a primer, then explodes the main powder in the shell and the shot goes rocketing out the barrel. The shot then travels at 1,300 feet per second or so toward the bird. All the time that this is going on, the muzzle is still moving ahead of the bird, increasing the amount of forward allowance, so that when shot leaves the barrel, the muzzles are well ahead of the bird, enough so that compensation is made for the human, mechanical, and shot flight-time. You send the dog for the retrieve.

All experienced shooters have had shots where the muzzles looked to be behind the bird when they fired—they didn't feel they caught up—but the bird came down anyway. This is the best proof that moving the gun continues to build the lead, even when you feel as though the shot is on its way. It's also the best reason to keep swinging, even when it seems unnecessary.

So much for short shots. Lead is largely uncomputed in the brain, even with fast birds—the faster the bird, the faster the swing, and the longer the lead.

Long shots, however, are a different matter. If the shot is at extreme range on a crossing bird with good speed, they can be tough to impossible—high doves, crossing pheasants, Hungarian partridge with the wind, and so forth. Waterfowl probably present the greatest challenge, because use of the less-than-optimum-efficiency steel shot means head and neck hits are necessary, which in turn means even more lead. How can we consistently make these long shots?

On such long shots, no matter how fast you swing, the amount of lead necessary just cannot, for most shooters in most situations, be allowed for by just quickly swinging the gun through. No matter how fast you swing, the lag time between the decision to shoot and shot leaving the barrel is not long enough to compensate for the greater distance. It works in close where little forward allowance is necessary; farther out, more lead is needed, and a fast swing won't work, at least it won't work consistently. Even Robert Churchill, famed British gun-maker and shooting coach who advocated no perceived lead, just a fast swing, said that on long shots it may be necessary to see some daylight ahead of the bird as you pass through before firing.

The answer to consistently making this shot, for some, may lie with the "moving spot" Nash Buckingham referred to over and over in his writings. In effect, this is a spot that takes the place of the bird. With long, crossing shots, the moving spot—not the bird—becomes the target. We execute the close-in, fast swing on the spot. So for practical purposes, we have doubled the lead. Shooting a bird-length ahead of the bird with a still or slowly moving gun isn't enough; swinging through and firing as you pass the bird isn't enough. So we must use both methods: a fast swing and then firing as the muzzles pass a spot that is ahead of the bird.

If you think of a spot a bird-length ahead of the target (more for smaller birds like Huns), and then execute the fast swing on that spot, you'll hit more than you'll miss. How far ahead the spot should be depends on you. People with fast reactions need a spot farther ahead because their "lag time," and therefore the amount of built-in forward allowance, is less. In other words, the longer it takes from the time your brain tells you to shoot until you actually do—provided the gun stays in motion—the greater the lead. What works out as right will depend upon you. But it's enough to say that fast-swinging through a moving spot will allow for a combination of leads that ought to put you where you need to be—up at the front end of the bird and still swinging.

What Is Good Shooting?

WHAT IS THE PURPOSE of shooting well? There are many, of course. To kill quickly and humanely is an altruistic one, one we should all adopt and hold to the highest level. To honor the dog with a successful point, flush, and retrieve is still another. To outshoot your buddy is a fine, respected goal—nothing wrong with it; I wish I could do it regularly. Or at all.

There are other motives—are you better on this bird or that one? Does this gun shoot better for you than another one? You may find out some strange things. For example, my notes show that I shoot better over pointing dogs (no surprise here because at least you've got a clue there's a bird nearby), but they also show I shoot better on wild bobwhites than on released birds. I have no idea why, other than maybe I'm on edge a bit more. You can be too relaxed.

So if we all agree it's better to shoot well than to shoot poorly, we have to define good shooting. Is there some sort of measuring stick against which we can place our rather pitiful averages? Well, I've got one, but it's highly subjective and comes from quizzing a lot of good shooters and pressing them to be honest (did you notice I was able to use both "shooters" and "honest" in the same sentence and I didn't stammer or even blink?). That yardstick is birds bagged per shells fired. If a pheasant flushes and you kill it with the second barrel, another flushes and you do the same thing, and a third flushes and you drop it with your first shot, you may be inclined to think you got three birds in three opportunities, and indeed you did. But, you shot three birds with five shells, which is 60 percent shooting. See how it works?

I admit it's tough to keep score accurately; we tend to give ourselves the benefit of the doubt. Every time. I stopped playing golf a couple years ago, at least regularly, because even though I know I was getting better thanks to some lessons from a friend, golf professional Brian Davis, my scores didn't improve. The reason, as my sons/playing partners pointed out, was I cheated so horribly for so long, that I never wrote down a real score. Now that I was recording the real thing, there was no change. See? Whoever said cheaters never prosper was talking about golfers. And shooters. And me, probably.

All things being equal, and they rarely are, such as normal weather conditions and good dog work, good shooting—according to good shooters—is pretty close to the following:

- Pheasants: two birds for three shells .67%
- Bobwhite quail: five birds for eight shells 62%
- Desert quail: three to four birds for eight shells . . . . .38% to 50%
- Ruffed grouse: two birds for five shells 40%
- Woodcock: three birds for five shells 60%
- Hungarian partridge: one bird for two shells 50%
- Sharptails/prairie chickens: five birds for eight shells 62%
- Doves: two to three birds for five shells . . . . .40% to 60%
- Ducks (over decoys): two birds for five shells 40%
- Ducks (pass shooting): one bird for three shells 33%
- Geese (over decoys): two birds for three shells 67%
- Geese (pass shooting): one bird for two shells 50%

A few disclaimers here: The biggest problem with waterfowl is making sure they are in range for the legally mandated steel shot. If you are using bismuth or tungsten shot, both of which have greater killing ranges and efficiency, you should shoot a bit better. With covey birds (quails and Huns), the averages quoted include a combination of covey rises and singles shooting. Finally, you may not hit these averages every time out, but it's okay to average your averages. If you go two-for-seven on quail one day, then follow it up with one of those red-letter days of eight for nine, you have averaged 62 percent.

If you can shoot like this, with all your guns, you don't need any more advice from me; you are hereby considered a good shot and you sure don't need to lie about it any more. Save that for your golf game.

Have You Ever Noticed?

Knowing What (Not) To Say

EVERY YEAR ACROSS the United States, hundreds of relationships are strained, dozens more damaged, a handful deteriorate into blows, and a couple here and there erupt into gunfire. The reason is because some folks don't know how to treat other folks' dogs. I mean, if The Battle of Gettysburg started over shoes, you can imagine what would happen if you offhandedly comment, "Your dog don't have a very damn good nose, do he?"

Now right off, most of us will admit that getting your dog to perform/behave/act semidomesticated in front of your shooting acquaintances is a little like the seven things Hercules had to do to get the girl. But that's not uncommon—your kids pull the same thing on you in front of company, probably. But, I mean, it's your dog, right? You should be the one that makes the decisions, administers the proper incentive, and calls the shots.

Each year, the pointing dog fraternity grows a little larger. Each year, people who have been hunting with either no dog or (gasp!) a flushing dog come into The Fold and over to The True Faith. Likewise. each year a lot of friendships are strained because the New Pilgrims know not how to deal with the other guy's dog.

So, in the interest of unity, harmony, and splendid days afield, here is a brief synopsis of things dogs are likely to do that the first-timer might find cause for alarm. This translates into wanting to assist the owner/handler, which has a tendency to result in the odd punch in the face. Instead, with a little preparation, you can come off looking great, be invited back, and maybe even get a gift puppy one day.

Now, right off, you have to understand some terminology when it comes to bird dogs, provided you haven't previously had the pleasure. Most of these terms deal with a dog's shortcomings, and so they shouldn't be used when the owner's around, even if he's in the next field. Dogs do strange things and some of these things go by strange names. The best thing to do is to try to find something good about each of these little behavioral nuances and comment on it. Hope this helps.

Wide-ranging

This refers to a dog that you met in the morning at the truck and you see him again two hours after dark tied to a tree in a farmer's yard 15 miles away. Such dogs are often described as "big-going," meaning from a standing start they're about three lengths and a nose ahead of a cruise missile. They thrill their owners who watch in wonderment as the dog is released and then seems to just sort of run away from home. Following on horseback is an option, provided you're riding Pegasus or a close blood relative of Secretariat.

Best Tip: Make references to the dog's "stamina."

Walking Too Close

Such dogs are always underfoot, finding birds you'd have flushed yourself in three more steps. They're usually timid, possess so-so noses, and are always around when you break out the sandwiches. Such dogs are normally the family pet, so any offside remarks will be taken badly.

Best Tip: Comment on the dog's pretty collar, fluffy ears, and his delightful need for human "companionship."

False Pointing

Simply, pointing a bird that isn't there. This is usually covered up by the owner maintaining that a bird had been there recently, and you should be ready because it's running. You look at the ground and see Old Fang eye-to-eye with a stink sparrow and know better. False pointers will point anything from the bird in your game bag to sugar beets that fell off a truck. They point chickadees, chipmunks, farm cats, and those aluminum For Sale signs the real estate guys tack to fence posts. Unfortunately, they also point the odd grouse or pheasant or quail, and you quit believing him after the first seven minutes. So, when the bird does materialize, you mostly miss, your host chortles, and your hatred for the dog grows like a thing alive.

Best Tip: Admire the dog's "style."

Gun-shyness

Some dogs flat don't like the sound of gunfire. They run and hide, generally, when things start getting noisy, and coaxing them out from under the truck can get to be a chore, especially when it happens three- or four-dozen times a day and you're a half-mile from the truck every time. You have an inkling when it's going to happen, at least, if you listen to the dog carefully. Normally, a gun-shy dog will moan softly, followed by a single, high-pitched, barely audible whine. This means, roughly translated, "Feet, don't fail me now!"

Best Tip: Tell the owner the dog has "a nearly human level of sensitivity."

Eating Birds

This habit is the most counterproductive to the entire hunting experience. The dog eats the birds you shoot, usually at a dead run as his owner is chasing him shrieking like a commodities broker. Every successful shot results in a foot race to the bird that the dog invariably wins because he has learned to ignore all the niceties of being steady to wing and shot and honoring—giving him a head start toward lunch.

Best Tip: Comment on the dog's "fresh breath."

It has been said, "Men trifle with their politics and they trifle with their careers, but they do not trifle with their sport." Try this: Walk into a tavern and announce, in this order:

1. "Anyone who voted for Clinton is a jerk";
2. "Anyone who dropped out of college is a loser";
3. "Anyone who spends time walking behind a bird dog is an imbecile."

See which one of those gets you punched in your mouth.

You see, when it comes to gun dogs, upland shooters and water-fowl hunters have never been wired up exactly like they should be—haven't been since *Canis familiaris* stopped being *Canis lupus* and moved into the family cave on this side of the fire—and probably up onto what passed for the Neanderthal version of the good sofa.

I know one guy who has a female setter that breaks point, chases birds, eats the few my pal manages to scratch down, and at nine years old hasn't quite got the housebroken thing mastered. He dotes on her. The same guy is just finishing up a divorce to his third wife; this one couldn't get the toothpaste cap drill right or something equally planet-splitting.

So, it stands to reason that if you aren't used to hunting with dogs, you should realize there are several types as I briefly mentioned earlier in the dog section. There are those that find and point game—pointing breeds; there are those that find and retrieve downed birds—retrieving breeds; there are those that find and flush birds for the gun—flushing breeds.

Now on any given day, each of these lines can become blurred. Dogs that are supposed to point will flush, those that are supposed to retrieve can flush and, rarely, point, and all of them are supposed to retrieve after a fashion, even though only the retrieving breeds will do it with any degree of reliability.

The lines become further blurred by the retrievers and the pointers being wrapped up into one package called the "versatile" dog of Continental extraction, which means the mutt will flush when he should point, point when he should be chasing, and eat downed birds like God's going to stop making them.

Then there's the type not often discussed: The Other Guy's Dog…a breed apart.

You see, there is something special about The Other Guy's Dog, and you have to realize that right off. And hunting with this beast is usually an exercise in self-restraint you could use to train for the Olympic Water-Torture Team. I mean, you can go to this man's house and he hands you his newborn son to fondle. You can turn up your lip, recoil and cringe, and mutter something like, "Get the little bleeper away from me—he's all sticky," and the guy will shrug his shoulders and pass the kid off to his wife. But comment after a couple of drinks that the guy's two-thousand-pound shorthair is cutting the circulation off to your knees after sitting on your lap for the last four hours, and he shows you the door. And I mean right now.

Take a pal of mine. He's got a mutt name of Sam—big English setter. Dog's a moron. Everybody knows it, including my pal, who must have got him as the result of a bet he lost or something. Or, maybe he's serving community service for kiting a check a few years back. That's the only explanation for the bond that exists between my buddy and this beast. Sam has two talents, the same two that are exhibited by English setters everywhere: eating and sleeping. Sam's world-class. Except, that's all he does.

Oh, my buddy takes him hunting, all right. Sometimes when I scrape up the nerve or I can't get out of it, I go with them. We hunt grouse and we hunt woodcock. Mostly, we hunt for Sam, who gets out of the truck and just sort of leaves. About every 20 minutes, my pal starts shrieking at Sam, takes off through the cover like he was catapulted, and tackles Sam, who is heading for the epicenter of magnetic north. They wrestle in the leaves for a bit, and my buddy wins because he's in better shape than Sam. Then, Sam hunts for awhile—maybe even points, although that's no guarantee he smelled anything or knows even a trifle more than we do about the whereabouts of any birds. Then, Sam splits again, and the scene is repeated.

But if you can stay with my pal when he goes after Sam, you'll get some shots, because the guy's the best flusher I ever hunted with. Hands down. Now naturally, I don't criticize old Sam. He's doing the best he can with what he's got, poor soul. And besides being cruel to the dog, criticism would have a tendency to set my friend's teeth on edge to the point that you can watch the enamel splinter. You see, he doesn't trifle with his sport, either.

Spotting a felon among the changing cast of characters you'll hunt with in a year is easy, once you know what to look for in The Other Guy's Dog. First tip: The name. Now, folks who run a lot of dogs over the years have sort of run out of names, so they give them people names: Fred, Bill, Sally, Poindexter—you know. A dog handler at a Southern plantation with 50 dogs doesn't have time to sit around and think up cutesy names.

But, our hero is different. The cuter, more autumn-is-the-smoky-colored-umber-smelling-earth-in-its-majesty sounding the name is, probably the worse the dog is. The inverse is usually true also; the simpler the name, the better the dog because he's been named and trained by a guy who ran out of those sweet little names 30 dogs ago.

There are exceptions (see "Sam" above) both ways, but it's a good starting rule of thumb.

For example, if your hunting pal introduces you to his new Lab "Misty Morning," ("Missy" for short), be ready for the canine equivalent of the Hillside Strangler. Good Labs are named "Maggie" and "Tar" and "Jake." If the man's chiseled-headed setter looks like an Osthaus painting and has a name like "October Delight," think about spending that particular Saturday in the Christian Science Reading Room.

There aren't many things I know too much about, but I learned a long time ago not to verbalize my true opinions of The Other Guy's Dog. You'll forgive me if I give you advice without informing you of the exact details that give me the right to give it. Trust me when I tell you it is hard-won knowledge I paid for in dashed friendships, bad hunting trips, and the temporarily rearranged facial feature. Innocent little remarks on my part, I tell you, but the opposition has no sense of humor.

So, for your enlightenment, here's the advice:

As I indicated earlier, you should develop an alternative vocabulary, commit it to memory, and use it when you discuss The Other Guy's Dog with him. Use these terms only when called upon. Volunteer nothing. To wit:

Good range. This means the dog can be actually seen on clear days if you're on one hill and he's passing over the next. Replaces previous usages, "coyote" and "smoker."

Thorough. This refers to the dog that thinks the birds are most likely found between your feet or eight yards behind you. Avoid here the use of the term "bootlicker."

Intensity. Another term you can use to admire The Other Guy's Dog. This is best used after you've had a tug-of-war to get a bird away from him. Substitute for "hardmouth" and "jarhead."

Good conformation. Use this when the dog at least seems to vaguely resemble any one of the following: the sire, the dam, the breed, a dog. Avoid at all costs discussions of "papers" and "Field Dog Stud Book."

Staunch. Admire the mutt's "staunchness" if you notice he has a tendency to doze off while on point.

Drive/Fire. These can be used interchangeably in referring to a dog who can't stay on the ground when birds are in the air. To The Other Guy,"steady to wing and shot"might as well be"byziliop nugerlow epilimbot."

People-oriented. This means the dog will spend at least a portion of what he considers down time in the field trying to hump your leg. Admire his friendliness. Comment on how he's "bonded" with humans. Kick him when The Other Guy isn't looking.

Puppysitting

A FRIEND OF MINE MADE the mistake the other day of leaving his six-month-old Labrador retriever puppy with me while he went out of town for a few days.

With the exception of a friend asking you to drop by the hospital and check to make sure his invalid mother's ventilator is still working, nothing is more presumptuous of your time than puppysitting a semi-trained male Lab, a Philistine in the best of times.

Now in situations such as this, you can rock back on your heels and look forward to several days of cleaning up surprises and not getting much sleep because the pup misses daddy, or you can make the most of it—an impromptu creative project handed to you by the gods.

Harper, for this is the name of the beast, is about what I expected from a male Lab of that age: mostly tongue, constant motion, and not what you would call gifted. My friend had done what he could to train him, with little apparent effect. I sensed that I could help.

First, it was painfully obvious to me that the dog did not have a clue about the proper procedure for table begging. Table begging is an important skill because we don't spend enough time at meals with family these days, and this is the time when we should relax and interact with one another. In table begging, the beggar must learn to patiently wait at the elbow of the begee, watching each morsel as it disappears down the well-known hatch in case something drops or—dare he hope?—that you will share. Of course, it's necessary to give the dog a little something, say a hamburger and a side of fries, now and then to keep his interest up. Good beggars can conjure up (or down) a string of drool at the drop of a fork. Harper caught on right off. It wasn't long until he'd progressed to the point of poking my leg with his nose or paw to remind me he was handy.

With that trick imprinted, we moved on to door greetings. Door greetings are important because our guests and stray visitors should be made to feel welcome and loved. You train for this by walking into the house through the front door with a piece of beef jerky in your shirt pocket. You pat your chest with both hands, gesture toward the jerky, and sharply holler, "Down!" When the mutt jumps up on you, paws on your chest, you give him the jerky and scratch his ears, all the while shouting, "Down, down, bad dog!" Amazingly, even slow-starters of mediocre breeding such as Harper will catch on quickly.

There were other tricks; it was a long weekend and I had time on my hands so I figured, "What the hell." There was the sleeping-on-the-couch trick, the finding-the-shoes-by-dragging-everything-out-of-the-closet trick, and the doing-the-bad-thing-on-the-potted-palm trick. Again and again, Harper was up to the challenge.

The upshot, if you haven't guessed already, is that I will never again be asked by my friend to puppysit. Or dogsit. Or babysit for his kids. Or feed his pet iguana. In fact, I haven't heard from him for a while, now. I should give him a call to see how the training's coming along.

Live Bird Competitions

I WAS READING ABOUT one of those pheasant championships the other day. I've got to tell you that I have a problem with game bird competition events. But I have less of a problem with some of them.

The oldest of these competitions, of course, is the live pigeon shoot, an honorable pastime in several countries. I'm not talking about those.

I dislike and refuse to participate in the so-called "one-box" this or that hunt, and the National Anything Hunt where "champions" are designated based upon body count. Where the resource (the birds) is wild and fragile, a slew of out-of-staters combing the coverts in search of birds to convert into laurels of glory and a trunkful of prizes reminds me of the "good fish, big fish" boys who chase bass for fun and profit.

The other kind, I have—make that had—no real opinion on. These hunts are for released birds on a preserve, and they involve some convoluted rules, require a good smattering of luck and the nerve of a double agent.

This one I got roped into was billed as a"Chukar Championship," and it involved released chukars, a 40-acre field, a finite number of shotgun shells, a fixed time period, a dog, and The Partner From Hell. I figured, with the off-season and all and nothing better to do...

The way the deal is, Partner and I and Partner's dog get 20 minutes total time, six shotgun shells each, and we are turned loose in a field that had a guaranteed six chukars in it. We got points for each bird the dog pointed, points for a retrieve, points for any time left from the 20 minutes, and points for any shells unfired.

Obviously, the way to win was to shoot quickly and well at pointed birds, and get all of them retrieved. Partner also told me that we could win, provided"I wanted it bad enough."

Now, I figured out right away that missing was a bad thing. For starters, you don't get the important retrieve points. You also use up shells (six-for-six being the perfect score) and time, what with the cursing and calling the dog back and all.

Partner is a dog expert: his dog is very good. I also quickly deduced that that would then make me the Hired Gun, brought along to take care of the six-for-six thing, and be right smart about it, too. Did I mention it cost us a hundred and fifty bucks to get into this thing?

I looked over the competition. Some of them were wearing running shoes, and they had their cuffs taped shut so they wouldn't catch on the grass and slow them up, I supposed. I didn't see anybody with a shaved head, but I wouldn't have been surprised. There were some bald guys, but I figured that didn't count. I knew they were serious, and it would take a lot of luck to avoid embarrassment.

The luck actually starts with the draw the evening before, in which our order of running was determined, just like a field trial. I didn't listen much to what was going on; there was a lot of rough talk and strong drink, all of this sounded vaguely like physics or something, so at the drawing mostly I zoned out. But Partner filled me in: A late draw is what you want, see, because there are six birds put out for every team. If the teams before you don't get all of their birds, that leaves more for us. If you're first, or all the teams ahead of you have been very efficient, there are only six for you. What you want is for all the other competitors to miss or not find their birds. If three teams ahead of you are sloppy, and you get six birds released, that makes maybe two-dozen chukars out there, which greatly increases the speed with which you can find and shoot six birds. He also told me that the real secret to winning was "wanting it bad enough." Hmmm.

There is a starting point, and once you pass it and are into the field, they start the clock. Now, I had been warned about the "gallery bird." This is a chukar that's planted—as if it would stay put—near the starting point. We're supposed to slide over to it, get a point, a clean shot, a retrieve, and then move on. The crowd—and there is one —gets to watch, and everyone's happy, provided we do everything right. It should be an easy bird.

Of course, our gallery bird must have found a mate and was off building a nest. The dog couldn't locate it for a couple of precious minutes. Finally we get a point, and we move in to flush. The bird takes off straight at the gallery. Even though neither of us raised our guns, we saw a little of everything from the folks in the crowd, who evidently figured we'd shoot—bugged-out eyes, sucked-in breath, people diving for the ground, and one SBR (Spontaneous Bladder Release) from an older gentleman wearing an eye patch.

So we're down one bird. The dog found another right away, and held until we got there. The chukar came off the ground and swung my way, crossing left to right at about 15 yards. I start to swing and just as I catch up, Partner screams "SHOOT!" which makes me twitch a bit and I miss. Twice.

I deduce that the gallery bird and my two-barrel whiff have mathematically eliminated us from any chance of a respectable finish. I am able to deduce this because Partner is screaming, "WE AIN'T GOT A CHANCE, SMITH, NICE GOING!"

The rest is a blur and mercifully forgettable. I think we ended up shooting one bird, had two fly away before we could get close enough for a point, and we never saw the sixth bird. My partner in this ill-fated endeavor has not spoken to me since and refuses to return my phone calls. I've decided to swear off such competitions forever.

This one, by the way, was finally won by two insurance salesmen from Hoboken who used a pointing Lab that, when he found a bird, just stood there and looked at the ground in front of him. The insurance guys had to tell the judge the dog was pointing because they're the only ones who could tell. They were using 12-gauge autoloaders with the barrels cut back to about 23 inches bored, of course, straight cylinder, and they were shooting an ounce and a half of nines. They wore running shorts, Nikes, and tight T-shirts even though it was 40 degrees. The way they moved, they could have made the finals of the AAU 440 relay.

I guess I just didn't want it that bad.

The Discussion

IT SO HAPPENS, FATE BEING what it is, that both of my sons got married awhile back in the same six-month period.

And fate again being what it is, it happened in the late 1990s when the mores of society had wobbled their way toward equality such that the parents of the groom split evenly the costs of the revelry with the parents of the bride, a phenomenon that, I assure you, was not in effect when my daughter married six years earlier.

But having made a lifetime's work of being in the wrong place at the right time, the right place at the wrong time, and the wrong place at the wrong time, but rarely if ever in the right place at the right time, I was not astonished nor even mildly surprised by this turn of events. I was, however, surprised by what ensued. It turns out that The Opposition has learned to lie.

My pal, Gene Hill, had one evening, in a long, malty conversation, shared with me his secret for smuggling guns (and dogs and fly rods and other stuff) in and out of his house. He did it by lying about the price. Not just a little point-shaving, either, but a big old whopper of a lie, a toe-curling, suck in your breath, go-see-Father O'Brien-right-away type of lie. Once his wife had caught on, Hilly had divulged his secret in a magazine column, but by then, I had adopted it and made it mine. And, lo, these many years, it has worked to perfection. Not because my wife didn't understand that I was lying, but because she *did.* You see, we speak in code—we use prices that anyone listening in would think we should be committed. Or go back to 1922 where we came from. We each understand exactly what the other one is saying. It's our version of fish stories: You believe my lie, and I'll believe yours. Let me show you what I mean.

Along comes these weddings, see, and one night I'm sitting in my favorite easy chair with a calculator doing the long division trying to compute the caterer's bill in light of what it was going to cost me to get an extra set of barrels made for my Scott (in case you're interested, you can get several sets of barrels made for the same price as one dinner for several hundred of your closest friends, minus booze).

Along comes the Old Storm and Strife and plops down on the couch across the room and clears her throat.

"Hruumph," says she. I look up and she fidgets a little and then says, "The boys [our sons] each want a live band instead of a disc jockey at the reception."

I say, "That sounds nice. I like live bands. How much?"

She looks me straight in the eye—without a hint of a blink or wink—and says, "Thirty dollars."

I ask, "Each or for both weddings?"

"Each."

I lean back a little in the chair and say, "Well, that's quite a bit of money. I mean, that's what they're getting for a VHE Parker these days. I had to save for a couple of months to get thirty dollars to buy one earlier this year."

"Yes, I know, but it's still cheaper than some of the other costs, like the thirty-five dollars the photographer is charging."

I look at her, but before I can say anything, she says, "Each."

"Well, it'll be tough, but we can do it; nothing but the best, I always say. I'll just delay getting that new Elhew pointer puppy next month—there's twelve dollars right there."

"Yes, and if we run into trouble, maybe you can sell one of your guns. That Fox 28-gauge shotgun you got last year for seventeen dollars would help. You might even be able to get twenty for it. You said it was really an investment, which was why you bought it."

That, of course, turned me cold inside, so I changed the subject. "Have you bought your Mother of the Groom dresses yet?"

"Why, yes, I have. I couldn't find what I wanted in my size, so I had them made. I picked out the material, and they'll be ready in a few weeks. I go for a final fitting tomorrow. The blue one was six dollars and the light green one for the spring wedding was only four-fifty. Before tax."

"Well, you're surely a thrifty little shopper. You've saved enough that I might be able to afford that Beretta Sporting Clays gun I've been saving for. I'd like to get it now while it's still fairly cheap. I've heard they're going to raise the price up to eleven dollars after the first of the year."

"Well, I think you should get it, then, and let me worry about covering the wedding costs. You've got a lot on your mind."

She gets up and heads for the kitchen, but just before she leaves the room, she turns and smiles sweetly: "It's so nice that you're understanding about all this extra expense."

"It's the least I can do, dear. After all, a boy's wedding day only comes around once."

Committing Golf

SHOOTING HAS BEEN compared to golf—I've compared it myself more than I would care to admit. Sporting clays has been called "golf with a shotgun" so often that it's become a cliché. Lots of shooters play golf —something to do in the off-season—and it beats hell out of fishing, especially flyfishing, which appears to be best accomplished by those with limp wrists.

I have long suspected some of my colleagues to be closet golfers, although none will admit it to me, even after they've been primed with strong drink. Nevertheless, little phrases such as, "Well, that's about par for the course" creep into their everyday speech patterns. One well-known writer of Scottish pedigree that I know is the exception, freely admitting that he plays golf and enjoys it.

The rest of us have a problem with golf. I think it's a temper deal. Like if you have one, you shouldn't play golf. Now, I don't have what you would call a chronically short fuse; I'm probably as moderate as anyone, taking the small setbacks and insults of everyday life in stride. Mister Even Keel, that's me. But golf turns me into a frenzied, seething abomination on the practice green.

I measure my shotgun shooting by shots per bird and carry a respectable if not lusty average on a variety of birds using a variety of guns (guns are like golf clubs, of course—you should have enough—yardage, distance, all of that). My rounds of golf are measured by three standards:

1. Number of balls lost (a"good" round is measured this way).
2. Number of clubs bent or hurled into any nearby body of standing water (a"so-so" round).
3. Number of pending court dates with other golfers assaulted by:
   a. golf balls driven into their party for slow fairway play;
   b. golf balls driven at the green they're still on because they insist on standing there filling in their scorecards instead of moving on so I can play, or;
   c. golf balls driven onto the green as they're wasting time marking eight-inch putts because that's what the pros do on TV. (This would be a"bad" round.)

Sometimes my sons play with me, under protest and only because I am exceptionally proficient at the paying of greens fees. They are good golfers —one was even on his university's golf team. After five minutes, they look at me with embarrassment, then disgust, then pity. They stop using the term "Dad," lest someone overhear. When I am old and in my sick bed and I see that look of pity in their eyes, I will look past them and into the shadows beyond for Dr. Kevorkian.

Plaguing the Gunsmith

As I write this, the shooting season has been over for some time now, and so I have been busily at work plaguing the living hell out of two or three hapless gunsmiths. It's what I do in the off-season. I like to think of it as a gift, like being able to sing on-key or paint or quickly learn foreign languages.

I called Tom, one of my favorite targets, the other day, disguising my voice to his wife so he'll take my call, of course, and when he comes on the phone, I ask him how much to bend the stock on a little boxlock 16. I only need about $\frac{1}{32}$ of an inch less drop, I tell him.

"Smith?" he says. "Is that you?"

"Uh—yes." I answer. "I think my Scott needs—"

Click. Dial tone.

We'd been cut off. Damn phone company. I hit redial (don't you just love technology?), but there's no answer, even though I let it ring maybe 40, 50 times.

I call back the next day and he answers it himself, and I pick the conversation up about where we'd left it when his phone went out of order: "—about a thirty-secondth of an inch less drop. How much to bend it and when can I get it back?"

There's this big sigh on the other end of the line, and he says, "Look, a thirty-secondth is nothing. If you want a thirty-secondth less drop, don't shave that morning."

"I tried that, and it's not enough. Besides, my whiskers don't grow that thick anymore. Or the hair on my head, either, come to think of it. How much to bend it and when can I get it back?"

"I'm not going to try to put a little bend like that in a stock. It would never take, and then you'd be all over me like you were three years ago when you sent me that stock that you said needed a sixteenth of an inch more cast. You about made me crazy before it was all done, and you couldn't tell the difference when I was done anyway. I lost my shirt on that one, and it didn't matter because you traded the gun away two weeks later."

I figure that's ancient history, so I say, "Okay, if you can't bend it, how about a new stock? How much to make it and when can I get it?"

"Oh no you don't," he says. "We did this once, too. You even drove out here and picked out the wood and I did the thing exactly the way you wanted, and when you got the gun back you said the grain wasn't right and so you wanted a new stock."

"The grain wasn't, you know, dark enough. You know I like dark grain. Besides, I paid you for it, didn't I?"

"That's not the point, the point is I had to do the stock twice because you didn't know what you wanted when you started, so I ended up making other clients wait so I could finish your second stock."

"And a great one it was, too, Tom," I says. Now, about the thirty-secondth at the comb—"

Dial tone.

I hang up the phone. Tom must be very busy right now, and stressed. Poor fellow. I grab the phone and call Doc, another gunsmith with whom I've dealt.

He picks up the phone after three rings. I say, "Doc, I've got a problem with a stock on a little boxlock—"

"Smith?" he says, "Is that you?"

Getting It Right

HAVE YOU EVER NOTICED that there are some things we never, ever, seem to get right?

Take folding a roadmap for example. A lot of folks don't know that the admissions exams at MIT involve the applicant being placed alone in a room and being given a roadmap to fold correctly within four minutes. Those who get it on the first try skip college and go straight to NASA.

I was thinking of this about a year ago as Dave Meisner, my hunting pal, and I were cruising through the high country of Montana headed for a mountain grouse hunt in the Bitterroots. We had Dave's fine pointer, enough of the right kind of guns, some camping gear. And a back seat full of wadded-up roadmaps. Eighteen of 'em.

This time of year, the season opening and all, points out that there are things we continue to have problems with, and there isn't enough of the right kind of stuff out there to solve these recurring and very real difficulties. Got a beef with your boss at work? So what? There's 16 hours a day you don't have to look at him. But, pal, get the thermos cap cross-threaded in a goose pit four miles from the car and the snow's whistling past...

Speaking of goose pits, I've also noticed I can't find a duck-hunting partner who sees the fun intrinsic in my blowing a fake highball and scrunching down in the blind while he's outside with his waders down to his ankles getting rid of his morning coffee.

And somebody ought to invent a gunsmith with a calendar. (I shouldn't pick on gunsmiths so much; the last time I did, I evidently offended some of them who took crayon in hand and wrote me what I'm guessing are snotty notes.)

How about how long to hang game? We can never get that right, either. Opinions range from hanging a bird until the head rots off, to meeting it with a roasting pan when it hits the ground after you shoot it. I mean, c'mon.

Or like properly putting a new finish on a shotgun stock. It's like trying to play solitaire with someone else around. It's a magnet. I always carry a deck of cards with me when I go into strange country. I figure if I ever get lost, I'll start playing solitaire. Before I get the first ace up, the rescue party will be gathered around me telling me to play the black nine on the red ten.

It's like that with the stock finish. Never, never tell anyone you're finishing a stock yourself unless you want instant company. The old Negro League baseball player, Cool Papa Bell, was said to be so fast he could turn out the light and be in bed before the room got dark. Bell was glacial compared to how fast your shooting pals will get to your place to tell you what you're doing wrong with the stock finish job. Linseed is waterproof. Is not. Is too. Not enough varnish. Too much varnish. Sand the varnish but don't rub it down. Rub the varnish down but don't sand it. What the hell are you using varnish for, anyway?

And the only charge for this advice is paid off by your liquor cabinet.

Try, for example, announcing that you just got a new pup and you plan to train it yourself. Wow. Your hunting buddies will manage to amble over during the yard training, help themselves to a cold beer from your refrigerator, plop down in one of your lawn chairs (in the shade), and while away the afternoon telling you what you're doing wrong and the names of good trainers who do this in exchange for money and quit being such a tightwad.

Finally, if they really cared about folks like us, they'd develop some type of course we could take or pamphlet we could read that would cure us of bragging before a hunt.

Think you're a passably good shot? Comment that you generally bring the left barrel home clean, and you'll get a solid week of covey rises in the greenbrier or mallards ahead of a force-five gale.

Got the idea you never get lost in the woods and you sort of let on to your partner that he shouldn't worry about finding the car when you come out? Better hope you didn't use up all your vacation time.

And if you should happen to allow that your new pup seems to not only be staunch on point but has pretty well got the quartering in gun range thing down pat, be prepared for him to be picked off and held for you as he passes through Canadian Customs.

Stuff I'll Do Differently the Next Time I Get a Puppy

MOST OF US DON'T HAVE the sort of bird dog we want, nor even a dog as good as we claim to other folks. But, like the rest of life, though we don't always get what we want, we usually end up getting what we deserve. The reasons are quite simple, really, and fall into three categories:

1. We don't know what we're doing;
2. We know what we're doing but we don't have the time to do it;
3. We have a pretty good idea of what we're doing, but the dog wins.

Regarding number 1, there are books—and a couple of good magazines (*The Pointing Dog Journal, The Retriever Journal*) to teach us what to do, so that's not much of an excuse.

Number 2, well, it doesn't really take that much time to train a dog; 10 to 30 minutes a day will produce a passably good one. They learn quickly, and you're dealing with instinct and heredity here. The dog wants to go hunting because that's what he's bred for. You just may have differing views on how the "go hunting" thing is going to happen.

Which leads to number 3.

All day long you work, using your intellect and abilities to solve the day-to-day problems and cope with the stresses of the workplace. When you come home at night, you want to relax a little, maybe play with the new puppy, do a little training so the dog will be what you want him to be come next fall. Visions of the two of you flit through your subconscious. There you are, leaning against a stone wall, puffing on your pipe. All around you the maples and aspens blaze with color, the sky the sort of blue that you could dab with a handkerchief. Your faithful pal lies at your feet, tired from a full day of serving you, his master, the Light of His Life. On the stone wall, not a feather out of place, is a brace of grouse and a woodcock, the results of three right barrels over cracking, tail-high points.

Not a chance.

Because while you were off fighting the mercantile wars, Wolfie was loafing all day, thinking up dirty tricks to play on you, all centered around the precept that, "If I pretend I don't know what he wants me to do, he'll eventually give up and I won't have to do it."

"Pointing," in dog parlance, becomes, alternately, "creeping," "sneaking," "bounding," or "pouncing," depending upon how close you are to the infraction and how much Muttly has caught up on his sleep. Retrieving becomes a contest bordering on the violent in which Sport gives up the bird only when he has mauled it to the point where you'll need dental records to tell if it's animal, vegetable, or mineral. As for the retrieving breeds, the thought of your dog "taking a line" from your hand signal to a downed bird, and then following it at your request and bringing the bird back quickly and efficiently is so outrageous as to be laughable.

So, the next pup I get, since my current juvenile delinquent appears to be already beyond redemption, I vow the following, on the slim off-chance that I may have done a thing or two wrong:

- The dog and I will not play tug-of-war with anything remotely edible, which includes, but is not limited to: birds, his food dish, weenies, my wife's geraniums, or my 13-year-old English setter.
- I will not allow my next dog to lie on my chest while I'm trying to watch TV, on my lap while I'm trying to write, or on what he considers his half of my pillow while I'm trying to sleep.
- I promise I will not encourage my dog to chase the neighbor's Siamese cat, and I certainly won't ever do it again when she's got relatives out on her patio for a Bar Mitzvah party.
- Speaking of which, I probably won't work my dog on water retrieves in her pool, especially at 6 a.m. before I leave for work.
- I'm not sure I'll keep live quail for training and smuggle them in the house when it gets cold out. The cage doesn't fit through the door so they sort of just run around. Also, If I plan to shoot these training birds, I probably won't give them names again, either.

- And this one, impressed upon me just this past weekend: I promise to do something about my dog leg-humping the house guests
  before it becomes an addiction.

Negotiations

THE OTHER DAY, WHILE I was clandestinely making out a sheet of specifications on a new custom gun I'd saved more than a few nickels and
dimes for, my wife waltzed into the room, glanced into my soul, and
asked me if I had bothered to join battle with the federal tax forms yet.

I said no that I hadn't, and further that the Rules of Engagement
hold that the perjury customarily commences on April 14. Besides, had
I not already survived two IRS audits with a combination of feigned
ignorance, a wide-eyed, gee-whiz demeanor, and a box of loose receipts
as bewildering as the Gordian Knot? You betcha, Sweetknees, says I.

She pointed out that "survive" was a relative term, and she remembered how I was a raving lunatic for two weeks before each audit, and
that the night before each, I cried myself to sleep, didn't I, tough guy?

Well, she had a point, because in my business, it is hard to tell,
sometimes, business from pleasure. The IRS seems to have the theory
that if it's fun, you shouldn't be able to make a living at it, and you sure
as hell shouldn't be able to deduct it. So as a result, each year when
I'm doing my tax forms, I keep this in mind and don't deduct things
I'm sure I'm quite capable of claiming, paying tax on my income, such
as it is, like a good American patriot.

Here's just a partial list of the stuff I didn't claim on my tax form
in the last couple years, and frankly, I think I'm cheating myself.

- My dogs. Even though I make what passes for my living as a dog
  magazine editor, I never had the nerve to plunge in and take the
  Doggie Deduction. I use my dogs for photo models and for hunting and I write stories about the hunts, but still, I got no guts at tax
  time. The theory here is that if a guy were the editor of a yacht
  magazine, would he be obligated by his employer to have a yacht?
  Probably not. Carried to the nth degree, if you work for *Psychology
  Today*, you aren't required by your employer to rent a neurotic.
- Whiskey.

- Life insurance, specifically the portion that covers the hours I spend hunting. If I hunt, say, 60 days a year, that's one-sixth of the year. I should be able to take one-sixth of the premiums as a deduction. After all, my chances of falling off a hillside into a canyon chasing chukars in Washington are much greater than having the water cooler fall on me at the office.
- Guns. I'd have to do something the IRS calls "depreciate" them. This, of course, flies in the face of the stories I've been telling my wife about how guns *appreciate* and that they're good investments. If she hears me griping about depreciating guns, well, that would just never do, would it?
- Gun safe. Along with the guns, of course, is the fire- and creep-proof gun safe I bought. Can't claim it—how do I deduct something that I bought to protect something I can't deduct? Even I can answer that one.
- Entertainment expenses. I gave up on this one—too much trouble. What are they? Can I declare the money I lose to Dave Meisner on shooting bets? I should—he's always entertained as hell. How about the money I annually lose in the duck camp poker game the night before the opener? It's as sure as the sunrise. Three years ago I couldn't make the opener or the game, so I mailed in eighty bucks and told the guys to divide it up just like always. What about the two hundred I lost at a little casino in South Dakota trying to teach my kid how to play blackjack? See? Where do you draw the line? Hunting licenses lead to hunting, which is entertainment; shotgun shells lead to shooting, which is entertainment; new boots lead to walking behind the bird dogs in south Georgia, which is entertainment. That's the problem—it's all entertainment, and don't let McIntosh, Bodio, or any of the others tell you any different. Maybe the IRS is right—you shouldn't be able to deduct it.